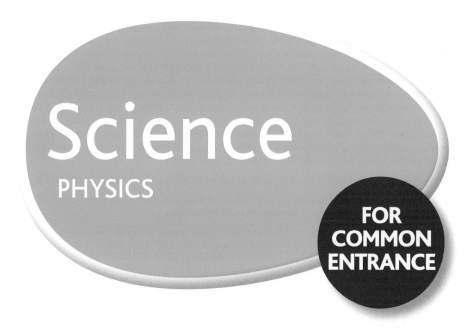

Science

PHYSICS

FOR COMMON ENTRANCE

Ron Pickering

GALORE PARK

AN HACHETTE UK COMPANY

The publishers would like to thank the following for permission to reproduce copyright material:

Photo credits

b = bottom, m = middle, t = top, r = right, l = left

Cover photo © iscatel - Fotolia **pvii** © Christian Schwier - Fotolia **px** © Romolo Tavani - Fotolia **pxi** © Donna - Fotolia **p1** © Jake Hellbach - Fotolia **p2** © Valeriy Velikov - Fotolia **p4t** © petert2 – Fotolia **p4b** © st-fotograf - Fotolia **p4mt** © mrcmos - Fotolia **p4mb** © apops - Fotolia **p10** © FirstBlood - Fotolia **p11t** © Stockbyte/Thinkstock **p11b** © Michael Gray - Fotolia **p14** ©Andriy Bezuglov - Fotolia **p17** © Brian Jackson - Fotolia **p18t** © william87 - Fotolia **p18b** © martin33 - Fotolia **p32t** © cristi180884 – Fotolia **p32b** © Andrey Armyagov – Fotolia **p35m** © ivanraul - Fotolia **p35b** © Xuejun li - Fotolia **p40** © Marc Xavier – Fotolia **p50** © AKIRA/amanaimagesRF/Thinkstock **p52, p54** © wojtek - Fotolia **p63b** © Science Photo Library **p63t** © Michalis Palis - Fotolia **p63m** © sergio37_120 - Fotolia **p86** © anyaivanova/iStock/Thinkstock **p87** © sumnersgraphicsinc - Fotolia **p90** © feelphotoartzm - Fotolia **p91** © Alexander Shevtsov - Fotolia **p94t** © spotmatikphoto - Fotolia **p94b** © Кирилл Рыжов - Fotolia **p99** © famveldman - Fotolia **p100t** © robertositzia - Fotolia **p100b** © pixelrobot – Fotolia **p102** © tsuneomp - Fotolia **p103** © apfelweile - Fotolia **p105l** © Elenathewise - Fotolia **p105r** © WavebreakmediaMicro - Fotolia **p106** © Andriy Solovyov - Fotolia **p109** © pat_hastings - Fotolia **p128t** © Les Cunliffe - Fotolia **p135t** © arenaphotouk - Fotolia **p136b** © sergio37_120 – Fotolia **p138** © iSailorr/Thinkstock **p147t** © Philippe Psaila/Science Photo Library **p147b** © Vacclav - Fotolia **p153** © markus dehlzeit - Fotolia **p156** © NASA/Science Photo Library **p158** © Beboy - Fotolia **p162** © Nicholas Piccillo - Fotolia **p166b** © NASA/Science Photo Library **p167** © Scrivener - Fotolia

p3, p29, p38, p51, p53, p80, p96, p113, p118, p128b, p130, p135m, p135b, p136t and p166t © Ron Pickering

Every effort has been made to trace all copyright holders, but if any have been inadvertently overlooked the publishers will be pleased to make the necessary arrangements at the first opportunity.

Although every effort has been made to ensure that website addresses are correct at time of going to press, Galore Park cannot be held responsible for the content of any website mentioned in this book. It is sometimes possible to find a relocated web page by typing in the address of the home page for a website in the URL window of your browser.

Hachette UK's policy is to use papers that are natural, renewable and recyclable products and made from wood grown in sustainable forests. The logging and manufacturing processes are expected to conform to the environmental regulations of the country of origin.

Orders: please contact Bookpoint Ltd, 130 Milton Park, Abingdon, Oxon OX14 4SB. Telephone: +44 (0)1235 827827. Lines are open 9.00a.m.–5.00p.m., Monday to Saturday, with a 24-hour message answering service. Visit our website at www.galorepark.co.uk for details of other revision guides for Common Entrance, examination papers and Galore Park publications.

Published by Galore Park Publishing Ltd

An Hachette UK company

Carmelite House, 50 Victoria Embankment, London, EC4Y 0DZ

www.galorepark.co.uk

Text copyright © Ron Pickering 2015

Impression number 10 9 8 7

2019

Typeset in 11.5/13 ITC Officina Sans Std/Book by Integra Software Services Pvt. Ltd, Pondicherry, India.

Printed in India

New illustrations by Integra Software Services Pvt. Ltd., Pondicherry, India.

Some illustrations by Graham Edwards were re-used. The publishers would be pleased to make the necessary arrangements with regards to these illustrations at the first opportunity.

A catalogue record for this title is available from the British Library.

ISBN: 9781471847042

About the author

Ron Pickering has published a number of very successful books covering the GCSE, IGCSE and A level syllabi and has worked in both maintained and independent education for more than 30 years. He now divides his time between teacher training, both in the UK and overseas, and writing, and has been a science advisor and curriculum manager at Altrincham Grammar School for Girls, as well as a Science Inspector for OFSTED.

Ron extends his interest in science by spending many hours photographing animals, both in the wild and in captive environments, and tries to maintain some level of fitness by off-road cycling.

Dedication

I dedicate this book to all young scientists, wherever they are, but especially to two microscientists, Noah and Kay, our beloved grandsons.

- Ron Pickering

Contents

Introduction

◯ About this book

Science for Common Entrance: Physics covers the Physics component of Science at Key Stage 3 and is part of an ISEB-approved course leading to 13+ Common Entrance.

In this book you will explore and investigate the physical processes that affect your everyday life. You will learn about the many forms of energy and how energy is transferred and conserved. You will continue your exploration of forces, learning about motion and speed, about rotation and simple machines and about pressure. You will also learn about waves – and discover more about the properties of light and sound. You will take a closer look at electricity, circuits and magnetism. Finally, you will learn a bit more about the movement of the Earth and how this gives us day and night and our seasons. You will learn about the Universe and about our exploration of our Solar System.

This book is part of a *Science for Common Entrance* series, which also includes *Biology* and *Chemistry*.

- *Biology*: In this book you will continue your exploration and investigations into the lives of plants and animals. You will learn something about the ways in which different living organisms, including ourselves, all depend on one another for survival; about how different organisms get their differences, and how they are passed on from generation to generation.
- *Chemistry*: In this book you will explore and investigate the properties of different materials. You will see that many of these properties are explained by the fact that materials are made of tiny particles.

Of course, scientists from the different areas of science work together so don't be surprised if you are asked to think about some Chemistry as you study Physics, or some Biology as you study Chemistry!

What do we mean by science?

As you go through this book you will continue to build on the scientific knowledge you have already gained. Remember that asking questions about the world around you is the first step to becoming a scientist. Carrying out experiments is a good way for scientists to start finding things out and to begin to answer some of the more challenging questions we have. You will already have got to grips with the idea of conducting fair tests when carrying out experiments and in this book we will give you the opportunity to do many more. You will also see some of the things we have found out from the results of experiments carried out by other scientists.

Notes on features in this book

Words printed in blue bold are keywords. All keywords are defined in the Glossary at the end of the book.

Sometimes you will see the heading **'Preliminary knowledge'**. The material in these sections is a reminder of facts or concepts that you should have learned at primary school. If any of this material is not familiar, take time to ask your teacher or read about the subject in books or online, before moving on.

> Useful rules and reminders and additional notes, looking like this, are scattered throughout the book.

> ### Did you know?
>
> In these boxes you will learn interesting and often surprising facts about the natural world to inform your understanding of each topic. Sometimes you will find a brief biography of an important scientist. You are not expected to learn these facts for your exam.

Working scientifically is an important part of learning science. When you see this mark you will be reading about the skills and attitudes you need to be a good scientist. You will find out:

Working Scientifically

- why we carry out experiments
- how to plan and carry out experiments
- how to evaluate risks
- how we ensure our findings are accurate and precise
- what we mean by the word 'variable'
- how to identify the independent, dependent and control variables
- how we measure variables
- what we mean by a fair test
- how to properly record and display results and observations
- how to spot patterns and draw conclusions
- how to calculate results, analyse data and use simple statistical techniques
- how scientific methods and theories develop as scientists modify explanations to take into account new evidence and ideas
- about the power and limitations of science and potential ethical issues.

Investigation

When we think like a scientist we might try to give some sort of explanation for what we observe. We might think that some mice are bigger than others because of what they eat.

In an investigation you will see a brief overview of how to carry out an experiment and how to record and interpret your observations in order to check out an explanation. Sometimes sample data is provided so that you can practise data analysis techniques, presenting data in graphs and charts and interpreting results and drawing conclusions.

The investigations given in this book are **not** intended as step-by-step instructions – your teacher or technician should provide these and carry out their own risk assessment if you are to carry out the investigation in the classroom. Do not try any of these investigations outside of the classroom without teacher supervision.

Exercise

Exercises of varying lengths are provided to give you plenty of opportunities to practise what you have learned. Answers are provided in the separate resource, *Science for Common Entrance: Physics Answers*.

Go further

When you see this heading, this highlights information that is beyond the requirements of the ISEB 13+ Common Entrance exam. You therefore do not need to remember the detail of this information for your exam, but it is helpful to understand the principles and applications of science described, in order to fully support your understanding of the subject area.

◯ What is physics?

One dictionary definition of physics is 'the study of matter and energy, and the interaction between them'. Physics describes many forms of energy – such as kinetic energy, electrical energy, and mass; and the way energy can change from one form to another. Everything surrounding us is made of matter and physics explains matter as combinations of fundamental particles that are interacting through fundamental forces.

Physicists ask really big questions like:

- How did the Universe begin?
- How does the Sun keep on shining?
- What are the basic building blocks of matter?
- Are matter and energy interchangeable?

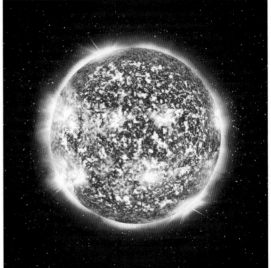

Many physicists work trying to find answers to these types of question and the answers they come up with often lead to unexpected technological applications. For example, much of the technology we take for granted today, including games consoles, smartphones, laptops and DVDs, is based on a theoretical understanding of electrons that was developed around the turn of the 20th century.

Physics doesn't just deal with theoretical concepts. It's applied in every sphere of human activity, including:

- Development of clean and environmentally friendly forms of energy generation. In addition, physicists investigate the most efficient ways of transmitting energy (from a power station to the laptop on your desk, for example).
- Maintaining health: radiotherapy in treating cancer, diagnosis of life-threatening medical conditions through various types of imaging and laser treatment of eye defects are all based on physics.
- Developing consumer electronics. The list is very long – plasma TV screens, touch-screen tablets, computer processors, portable media cards for digital cameras and laser reading of DVDs, for example.
- Construction of buildings, roads and bridges. Physics applies to building design and architecture in a number of ways. Firstly, it helps determine the entire basic structure of a building because physics helps to predict the best way to support weight and maintain stability. Secondly, physics helps us understand which materials are most affected by heat, light, and water. By studying how vibrations affect different structures, engineers are able to design buildings that can withstand natural disasters like earthquakes and hurricanes and also be maintained with the minimum expenditure of energy.

- Design and manufacture of sports equipment. It is no surprise that Dave Brailsford, the extremely successful manager of the Sky cycling team, employs physicists and engineers to study how to make the lightest, most efficient bicycles. Similarly, Lizzy Yarnold, a gold medalist at the Winter Olympics, has to have a team that understands how to produce a skeleton bob that is strong and will slide rapidly over ice.

- The exploration of space. The NASA expeditions to the Moon, and the recent journey of the spacecraft Rosetta leading to the landing of Philae on a comet are certainly applications of physics. So too has been the development of astronomical telescopes to provide us with information about the space beyond the Earth.

So, the applications of physics are everywhere: Physics is amazing!

Investigations in science

Before we launch into this book it is worth pausing and taking some time to go over some of the rules we need to follow in order that we can carry out experiments in a reliable way. These rules apply whether you are studying biology, chemistry or physics.

What is an experiment?

Every day we make hundreds of observations; for example 'more sugar dissolves in warm water', 'that car is moving faster than the other one', 'that tree looks bigger today' or 'some of the pet mice are bigger than the others'.

When we think like a scientist we might try to give some sort of *explanation* for what we observe. We might think that some mice are bigger than others because of what they eat. We might think that one sunflower is taller than the one next to it because it is getting more sunshine. Before it is proven, we call this explanation a **hypothesis**.

An **experiment** is a way of collecting information to see whether our hypothesis is correct. Before a scientist begins an experiment, he or she will have a definite **purpose** or **aim**. The aim of an experiment is a way of stating carefully what you are trying to find out. For example, 'My aim is to investigate the effect of voltage on current flowing through an electrical component'. Not just, 'Studying current flow' or 'Changing the voltage in a circuit'.

What about variables?

An experiment has the aim of investigating the effect of one factor (voltage applied to an electrical component, for example) on another factor (current flow, for example). These factors can have different values, and so are called **variables**. In our experiment we can change the **values** of these variables, so we might apply a greater voltage to one component than we apply to another. Anything that we can measure is a variable.

The experiment must be a fair test

Here are the steps you should follow before conducting an experiment:

Step 1: Write down your hypothesis and identify the variables. (Variables are factors that might affect the results.)

Step 2: Choose which variable you will change. This is called the **independent (input) variable**.

Step 3: Choose the variable that you think will be affected by changing the independent (input) variable. This is called the **dependent (outcome) variable**.

Step 4: Decide what equipment you will need to measure any changes. Then go ahead and carry out your experiment.

You are trying to find out whether the change in the independent variable causes a change in the dependent variable.

An experiment will not be a **fair test** if you change more than one variable at a time. To make sure that the experiment is a fair test, you will need to check that none of the other possible variables is changing.

For example, in the experiment investigating the current flow through a component, it is possible that the current flow might be affected by any of the following factors:

- the temperature
- how thick the connecting wires are
- the size of the component
- how long the connecting wires are.

These are the variables. If you want to investigate how voltage affects the current flow, voltage is your independent (input) variable, current is you dependent (outcome) variable and all of the other variables **must stay the same**. These are called the **control variables**.

Finally, remember to **work safely**.

- Always wash your hands after touching plants or animals.
- Carry equipment carefully.
- Don't run in the laboratory.
- Wear suitable clothing.

How we measure variables

Scientists like you need special equipment to measure any changes in variables. Some of these pieces of equipment, and what you would use them for, are described here.

Measuring length using a ruler

A ruler can be made of wood, metal or plastic. Along the length of the ruler is a numbered scale. One of the benefits of a plastic ruler is that it is usually transparent, so the object to be measured can be seen through it. The following diagram reminds you how to use a ruler.

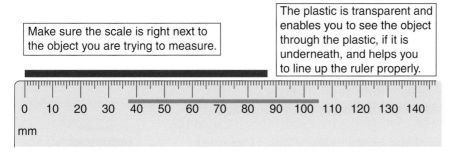

Make sure the scale is right next to the object you are trying to measure.

The plastic is transparent and enables you to see the object through the plastic, if it is underneath, and helps you to line up the ruler properly.

0 10 20 30 40 50 60 70 80 90 100 110 120 130 140

mm

Try to get the object up against the 0 on the ruler.

1) How long is the red line in millimetres (mm)?
2) How long is the blue line in millimetres (mm)?

Measuring volume using a beaker or a measuring cylinder

Beakers and **measuring cylinders** can be made out of glass or plastic. Scientists now often use plastic because it is less likely to break and so is safer. However, plastic beakers can't be used to boil liquids because they would melt and become distorted and useless.

The following diagram shows you how to use a measuring cylinder and a beaker.

| **Beaker** It is not accurate to use a beaker because the scale is not fine enough. | **Measuring cylinder** | Make sure the liquid is level. To do this, stand the measuring cylinder on a level table or bench. |

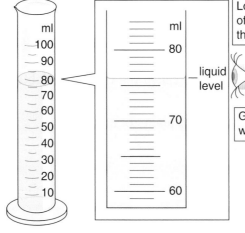

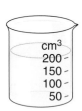

Look at the 'flat' part of liquid level, not the curved part.

liquid level

Get your eye level with the liquid level.

Is it cm³ or ml? Some equipment is scaled in cm³ and some in ml. It really doesn't matter – 1 cm³ has exactly the same volume as 1 ml.

Measuring other things

There are other things that scientists want to measure. These include temperature, force and mass. Measuring force is described in Chapter 3. Measuring current flow is also described in this book – see Chapter 9.

Measuring mass using a balance

Mass is the name scientists give to the amount of a substance. You can use a **balance** (also called a **weighing machine** or **scales**) to measure the mass of something. It is very important to remember that if you are weighing liquid in a container, you must subtract the weight of the container. You can do this as follows:

Step 1: Weigh the empty beaker. Note down its mass.
Step 2: Add the liquid and weigh the beaker again. Note down this mass.
Step 3: Subtract the mass of the empty beaker (Step 1) from the mass of the beaker containing liquid (Step 2).

An empty beaker

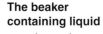

Balance (weighing machine)

The beaker containing liquid

Measuring temperature using a thermometer

Temperature is a measure of thermal energy or heat. Temperature is measured using a thermometer. Traditional thermometers have a thin glass or plastic tube that is filled with a liquid (liquid mercury or more often now a coloured alcohol). These liquids expand when heated and contract when cooled. Numbers are placed alongside the tube that mark the temperature when the liquid is at that level. Today we also have very accurate digital thermometers – see Chapter 1 for more information about how these work.

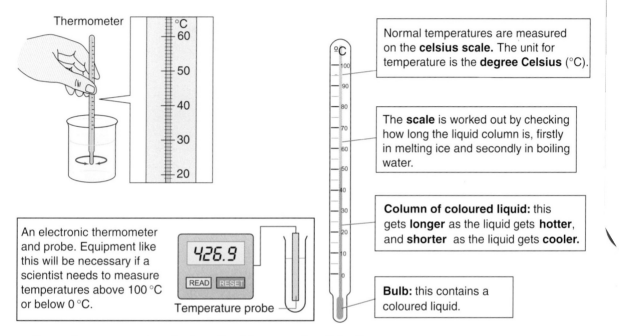

Normal temperatures are measured on the **celsius scale.** The unit for temperature is the **degree Celsius** (°C).

The **scale** is worked out by checking how long the liquid column is, firstly in melting ice and secondly in boiling water.

Column of coloured liquid: this gets **longer** as the liquid gets **hotter,** and **shorter** as the liquid gets **cooler.**

An electronic thermometer and probe. Equipment like this will be necessary if a scientist needs to measure temperatures above 100 °C or below 0 °C.

426.9

READ RESET

Temperature probe

Bulb: this contains a coloured liquid.

Measuring temperature is described in more detail in Chapter 1.

The table gives you a summary of measuring equipment and their uses:

■ Measuring equipment for use in science

Equipment	What it measures	Units (symbol)
Force meter	Force (and weight)	Newtons (N)
Balance	Mass	Grams (g) and kilograms (kg) 1000 g = 1 kg
Stopwatch or stopclock (analogue or digital)	Time	Seconds (s) and minutes (min) 60 s = 1 min
Measuring cylinder or beaker	Volume	Millilitres (ml) and litres (l) 1000 ml = 1 l
Ruler/tape measure	Length	Millimetres (mm) and metres (m) 1000 mm = 1 m
Thermometer	Temperature	Degrees Celsius (°C)

Exercise 1: Made to measure

Measuring cylinders and beakers are made from either glass or plastic.
1 Give two reasons why glass and plastic are useful materials.

2 Give one reason why glass is more useful than plastic when making measuring equipment.

3 Give one reason why plastic is more useful than glass when making measuring equipment.

Extension questions

4 Look at these diagrams. A scientist has measured the mass and the volume of some water and some alcohol. What can you tell from the measurements?

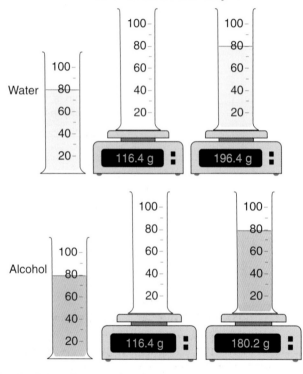

5 Minnie is going on a four-hour journey and she wants to take some water. She has a water container that weighs 120 g. She doesn't want to carry more than 260 g altogether. She would normally drink about 200 ml in four hours.
(a) What is the maximum mass of water she should take with her?
(b) What volume of water will this be? Will she have enough for her journey?
      Hint: 1 ml of water weighs 1 g.

Making a record of our results

Results (or **observations**) are a record of the measurements you have taken during an experiment. There are certain rules about the way you should show these results. They should be recorded in a table, like the one shown below:

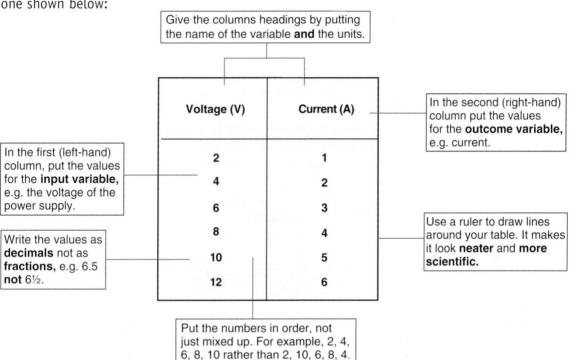

Give the columns headings by putting the name of the variable **and** the units.

In the first (left-hand) column, put the values for the **input variable,** e.g. the voltage of the power supply.

Write the values as **decimals** not as **fractions,** e.g. 6.5 **not** 6½.

Voltage (V)	Current (A)
2	1
4	2
6	3
8	4
10	5
12	6

In the second (right-hand) column put the values for the **outcome variable,** e.g. current.

Use a ruler to draw lines around your table. It makes it look **neater** and **more scientific.**

Put the numbers in order, not just mixed up. For example, 2, 4, 6, 8, 10 rather than 2, 10, 6, 8, 4. If you do, it makes it much easier to see patterns in your results.

When you look at your results, you may see a certain pattern. It might seem that the greater the voltage that is applied, for example, the larger the current flow.

Your results will be more reliable if you carry out each test more than once, and then take an **average** (mean) of the results. Why? You might just have chosen one component that doesn't work in a normal way. If you do the experiment with ten of the same components and work out the average weight, the results will be more **reliable.**

The mean is calculated by adding together all your results and dividing by the number of repeats. For example, the mean of 3, 2 and 4 is:

$$\frac{3 + 2 + 4}{3} = 3$$

If one or two of the results don't fit the pattern, the first thing to do is check your measurement. If your measurement was accurate, and you have the time, you can **repeat** the test to check the 'odd' result.

Displaying your results

Sometimes you can see a pattern in your results from the table you have made, but this is not always the case. It often helps to present your results in a different way. **Charts** and **graphs** display your results like pictures and they can make it very easy to see patterns, but only if they are drawn in the correct way. There are rules for drawing graphs and charts, just as there are rules for putting results into tables.

- First of all, look at the variables you measured. If both of the variables have numbers as their values, you should draw (sometimes we say 'plot') a **line graph**. If one of the variables isn't measured in numbers, you should choose a **bar chart**.
- You should always put the **independent (input) variable** on the **horizontal** (x) axis and the **dependent (outcome) variable** on the **vertical** (y) axis. If you don't do this, you can easily mix up the patterns between the two variables.

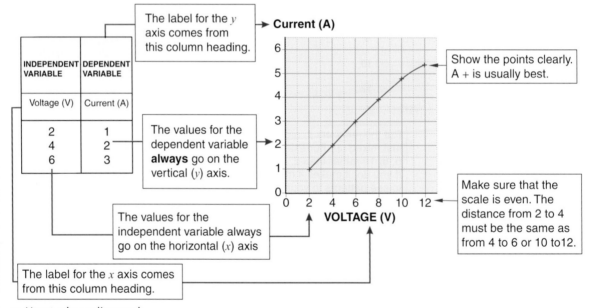

■ How to draw a line graph

The title of this graph should be: 'The effect of the applied voltage on the current flow through and electrical component'. The simple rule is: 'Effect of (independent variable) on (dependent variable)'.

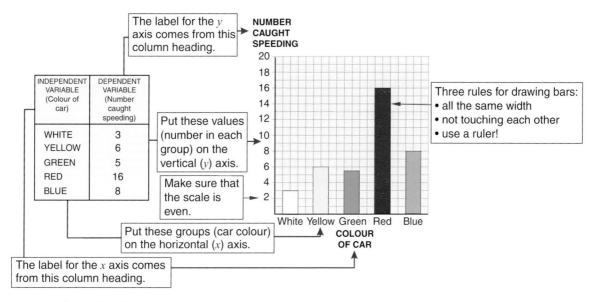

The label for the y axis comes from this column heading.

INDEPENDENT VARIABLE (Colour of car)	DEPENDENT VARIABLE (Number caught speeding)
WHITE	3
YELLOW	6
GREEN	5
RED	16
BLUE	8

Put these values (number in each group) on the vertical (y) axis.

Make sure that the scale is even.

Three rules for drawing bars:
• all the same width
• not touching each other
• use a ruler!

Put these groups (car colour) on the horizontal (x) axis.

The label for the x axis comes from this column heading.

■ How to draw a bar chart

In this case the title should be 'The effect of the colour of the car on the number caught speeding.'

Using graphs

A graph can let you see a pattern between two variables. For example, as voltage increases, so does the flow of current. The graph can also let you make **predictions** if it shows an obvious pattern. So, you might be able to predict how much current would flow if the voltage were to be increased by a certain amount.

Just before we look at how to do this using a graph, it is worth making an important point about predictions. It can be very useful indeed to make some of your own predictions even *before* you get started on your experiment. If you do this, it can help you to plan much better experiments. If we take the example of looking at the effect voltage has on the flow of current, we can make a pretty good guess (a prediction) that the greater the voltage applied the larger the measured current will be. We can also start to plan what apparatus we will need and so on.

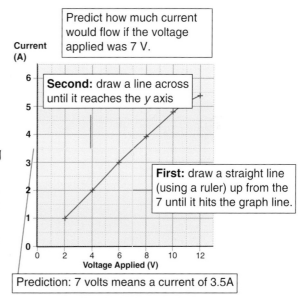

Predict how much current would flow if the voltage applied was 7 V.

Second: draw a line across until it reaches the y axis

First: draw a straight line (using a ruler) up from the 7 until it hits the graph line.

Prediction: 7 volts means a current of 3.5A

■ The effect of the voltage on the current flow through an electrical component

Making conclusions

Once you have collected all of your results into a table, and perhaps drawn a graph or chart, you need to sum up what you have found out. This summing up is called a **conclusion**, and here are some tips:

- **Your conclusion should be related to the aim of your experiment.** If your aim was to investigate the effect of voltage on current flow through an electrical component and you saw a clear pattern, then your conclusion might be that 'the higher the voltage the larger the current flow through a component'.
- **Try to write your conclusion simply.** One sentence is often enough but make sure it explains how the independent (input) variable affects the dependent (outcome) variable for your experiment.
- **Don't just describe your results.** For example, in an experiment on voltage and current the statement 'a big voltage increases current flow' is really giving only one of your results. A much better conclusion would be 'the current measured is proportional to the voltage applied'.

1 Energy changes and transfers

◯ What is energy?

Nothing can happen without energy. You use energy when you lift a mobile phone to your ear and the mobile phone uses energy to send a message. Energy is used whenever a force makes something move. The more energy that is used, the greater the force generated and the further something is moved. Energy is used to heat things up; the tiny particles that make up all matter move faster when they are given more energy. Many scientists would say that life depends on using energy. Once the body cannot use energy to keep all its molecules in the right places, then the body is dead! All these different things that energy is used for are examples of work. So, we could define energy like this:

Energy is the measure of:

- **work** that **has been done**
- **work** that **is able to be done.**

There are different forms of energy

Energy can take different forms, including chemical, electrical and thermal. Each is described below.

Chemical energy

The energy stored in a food (see Biology, Chapter 2), a fuel (see Chapter 2) or in an electric cell (a battery; see Chapter 9) is chemical energy. The energy is released during a chemical reaction (burning, for example – see Chemistry, Chapter 7).

Electrical energy

Energy that is due to electrical charges moving is called **electrical energy**. For example, electric current in a wire.

> Electrical energy is the most convenient form of energy, because it is so easily converted into other forms, and because it can be transmitted over long distances by wires.

Thermal energy

Energy due to fast-moving particles in hot objects is called thermal energy. For example, thermal energy is transferred from the open fire to the room and the people sitting in it.

Chemical energy

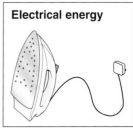
Electrical energy

Thermal energy

In addition to **chemical, electrical** and **thermal energy**, there is:

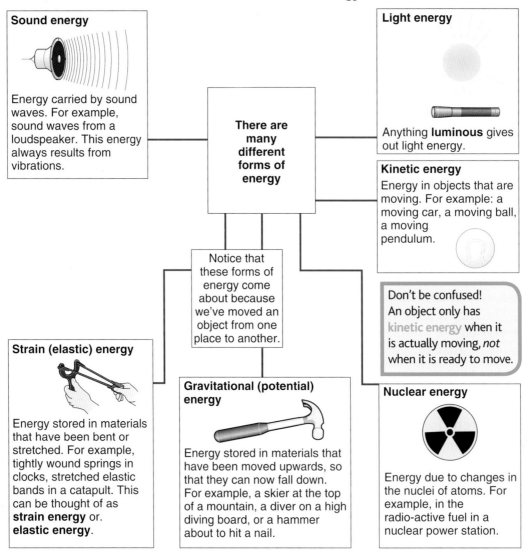

Sound energy

Energy carried by sound waves. For example, sound waves from a loudspeaker. This energy always results from vibrations.

There are many different forms of energy

Light energy

Anything **luminous** gives out light energy.

Kinetic energy

Energy in objects that are moving. For example: a moving car, a moving ball, a moving pendulum.

Notice that these forms of energy come about because we've moved an object from one place to another.

Don't be confused! An object only has kinetic energy when it is actually moving, *not* when it is ready to move.

Strain (elastic) energy

Energy stored in materials that have been bent or stretched. For example, tightly wound springs in clocks, stretched elastic bands in a catapult. This can be thought of as **strain energy** or. **elastic energy**.

Gravitational (potential) energy

Energy stored in materials that have been moved upwards, so that they can now fall down. For example, a skier at the top of a mountain, a diver on a high diving board, or a hammer about to hit a nail.

Nuclear energy

Energy due to changes in the nuclei of atoms. For example, in the radio-active fuel in a nuclear power station.

These different forms of energy do not just vanish when they are used. Energy can be changed from one form into another; this is called the transformation of energy and this is another way energy can be transferred.

An everyday example of transforming energy is shown below:

① Respiration releases chemical energy from food.

② An athlete gains movement (kinetic) energy.

③ An athlete gives out thermal energy.

Units of energy

The standard unit of energy is the joule (J). One joule isn't really very much energy and the number of joules used to carry out a particular piece of work might be very large, so larger amounts of energy are usually measured in **kilojoules (kJ)**. 1 kJ = 1000 joules. Here are some examples of different amounts of energy:

Typical energy values	Joules	Examples
Strain/elastic (potential) energy: Stretched rubber band	1 J	
Gravitational (potential) energy You, on top of a stepladder	500 J	
Kinetic energy: Kicked football Small car at 70 mph	50 J 500 000 J	
Thermal (internal) energy: Hot cup of tea	150 000 J	
Chemical energy: Torch battery Chocolate biscuit Litre of petrol	10 000 J 300 000 J 35 000 000 J	

> How many kJ of energy are there in 10 litres of petrol?

Energy chains

Energy can be transformed from one form to another. These changes of energy are sometimes called **energy chains**. In every energy chain the **total amount of energy stays the same** even though the energy is **changed from one form to another**. Scientists have measured many different examples of these energy transformations and have written down their observations as the Law of Conservation of Energy:

> Do you remember food chains in biology – the flow of energy from one living organism to another?

Energy cannot be made or destroyed but it can change from one form to another.

i.e.

the total amount of energy at the start = the total amount of energy at the end

Here is an example of an energy chain:

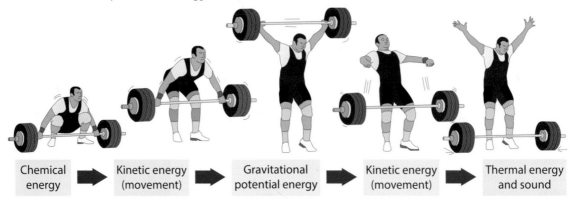

| Chemical energy | ➡ | Kinetic energy (movement) | ➡ | Gravitational potential energy | ➡ | Kinetic energy (movement) | ➡ | Thermal energy and sound |

Some energy is always transferred or 'lost' to the surroundings as thermal energy. For example, you get hotter when you convert chemical energy to kinetic energy when you exercise.

Living things, machines and electrical appliances transform (convert) energy from one type to another.

Describing energy changes

Energy is transformed when it changes from one form to another. For example, an electric kettle can transform electrical energy into thermal (internal) energy. A simple way to write down these changes is shown here:

electrical energy ⟶ kettle ⟶ thermal energy

This means that electrical energy is transferred to the kettle.

This means that energy is transferred to the water as thermal (internal) energy.

Anything that can change one form of energy to another is called a **transducer**. Many machines are transducers. Machines use energy to carry out work.

◯ Electricity

Electricity is a very useful form of energy. It doesn't produce pollution when it is used, it is easy to control and easy to send from one place to another using wires.

When we use electricity, we often change it into another kind of energy, using an electrical appliance as you saw in the example of the kettle.

An electrical appliance, such as those shown on this page, can transform electrical energy into another form of energy that is useful to us.

■ The electric fire changes electrical energy into **thermal** and **light** energy

■ The lamp changes electric energy into **light** and **thermal** energy

■ The television changes electrical energy into **light**, **sound** and **thermal** energy

■ The food mixer changes electrical energy into **movement**, **sound** and **thermal** energy

Think back to the idea of energy chains. You should be able to follow a chain of energy from the Sun to an appliance, such as a laptop monitor, as shown here:

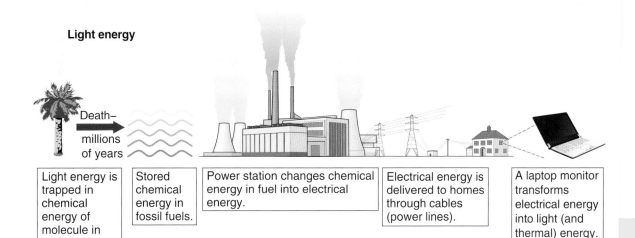

Light energy

| Light energy is trapped in chemical energy of molecule in plants. | Stored chemical energy in fossil fuels. | Power station changes chemical energy in fuel into electrical energy. | Electrical energy is delivered to homes through cables (power lines). | A laptop monitor transforms electrical energy into light (and thermal) energy. |

■ Energy chain: From sunlight to computer images

Working Scientifically

Investigation: Energy transformations

In these experiments you will be investigating examples of situations where energy is transformed.

Safety: You must wear safety goggles when striking the match. Take care when striking the match – it may burn you.

Remember that energy can change from one form into other forms. When this happens the total amount of energy stays the same.

No energy is lost, although some of the energy may go to waste (forms that we were not intending to have!).

Energy cannot be created from nothing.

1 Copy and complete the table as you carry out the investigations.

1. Rubbing hands	When your hands are moving they have kinetic energy. KINETIC ENERGY	What kind of energy does the rubbing produce?	Where did the energy come from for you to be able to rub your hands? ....
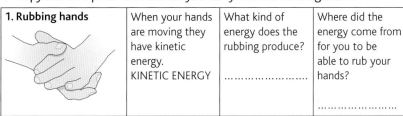			

2. Shaking a tin of nails	What kind of energy are you giving to the tin?	What kind of energy is this being changed into? .... and	
3. Striking a match	What kind of energy is stored in the head of the match?	What kind of energy is produced? .... and	What kind of energy starts off the reaction? ....
4. Clockwork timer	When the timer is wound up, what kind of energy is stored in the spring?	What kind of energy is then produced?	
5. Hairdryer	What type of energy is delivered to the hairdryer from the socket?	What two types of useful energy are produced by the hairdryer? .... and	What form of unwanted energy is produced? ....
6. Dropping masses Lift the mass above the sand and drop it.	What energy has the mass got just before you let go?	What energy has the mass got just before it lands?	Extension: What happens next to this energy? ....

1 Complete these paragraphs, using words from this list: You may not need to use all the words.

| energy | elastic | light | kinetic | transformed |
| joules | electrical | work | thermal | machine |

(a) To carry out any action, _____ is needed. All of these different types of action can be called _____. Energy comes in different forms. For example, _____ energy is stored in materials that have been stretched or bent. _____ energy is the energy of movement. _____ energy is the result of fast-moving particles in hot objects.

(b) Energy cannot be created or destroyed, but it can be _____ from one form to another. For example, a torch changes _____ energy into _____ energy. Energy is measured in units called _____.

2 A fire gives out 20 kJ of energy. How many joules is this?

3 A machine is a device for doing work. Use this list of machines to complete the table below:

match   radio   catapult   toaster   fan   motor car

Machine (transducer)	Energy is changed from	to (mainly)
	Electrical	Sound
	Electrical	Thermal
	Electrical	Kinetic
	Chemical	Kinetic
	Strain (elastic)	Kinetic
	Chemical	Light

4 Describe the energy changes that take place when you:
(a) throw a ball up into the air
(b) pull on the brakes of your mountain bike.

Extension questions

5 This question deals with electrical appliances that you could find in your home or school. Make a list of ten different appliances and use the list to complete a table like this one.

Appliance	Is it powered by mains or battery?	It converts electrical energy to ...	Some electrical energy is wasted as...

6 Scientists say that energy can never be created nor destroyed. Explain what they mean, and say whether you think this statement is true or not.

Temperature and energy

In the previous section you learned that no action can take place without energy and that there are different forms of energy. You also learned that energy can be changed or transformed from one form to another and that these changes always involve thermal (internal) energy. In this section you will learn more about thermal energy.

What do we mean by temperature?

Remember that thermal (internal) energy is just one kind of energy. If a material has a lot of thermal energy, we say it is **hot** and, if it has very little thermal energy, we say it is **cold**. Temperature is a scale of numbers that we use to measure the amount of thermal energy that a material has.

During your chemistry studies, in the section on dissolving solids (Chemistry, Chapter 2), we saw that we can dissolve more sugar in hot water than we can in cold water.

Working Scientifically

Rather than just saying 'hot' it would be better to give an actual number or measure of 'heat'. What feels like hot to one person may not feel quite so hot to another person. For this reason, scientists measure the temperature of the water using a piece of equipment called a thermometer when they are doing an experiment such as this. So, every person who measures the temperature of the same hot water, using a thermometer, should get exactly the same number. Refer back to the 'Investigations in science' section for more information about thermometers.

Gabriel Fahrenheit

Gabriel Daniel Fahrenheit (1686–1736) was a German physicist and glassblower. He invented the mercury-in-glass thermometer in 1714.

In 1724 he used his mercury thermometer to develop a temperature scale now known as the **Fahrenheit** scale. Gabriel Fahrenheit decided that the zero on his scale (0 °F) would be the lowest temperature he could reach; this was the temperature of the freezing point of the strongest salt solution he could make. He also decided that 100 °F would be the temperature of our bodies.

The Fahrenheit scale has been further developed and refined over time. For example, work by other scientists showed that water boils about 180 degrees above its freezing point, and so the Fahrenheit scale was redefined to make the freezing to boiling interval exactly 180 degrees. This redefinition means that body temperature today is read as 98.2 °F.

Working Scientifically

By the end of the twentieth century, most countries, including the UK, had switched to using the Celsius scale (see below), but Fahrenheit continues to be the main scale for temperature in the USA.

Anders Celsius

Anders Celsius (1701–1744) was a Swiss astronomer and physicist. In 1742 he developed a different temperature scale. His scale was based around the freezing point and boiling point of pure water, with a hundred degrees between them. The freezing point of water is therefore given as 0 °C and the boiling point as 100 °C. This scale is now known as the **Celsius** scale, but Anders Celsius originally called it the centigrade scale, from the Latin for 'hundred steps'.

The Celsius scale is the main scale for temperature in most countries and it is used in many scientific applications.

Did you know?

There is also another temperature scale used in science, called the **kelvin** (K) scale. This scale was developed by many scientists in the mid-twentieth century and named after Lord Kelvin (William Thomson, 1824–1907), who was the first to state and determine the lowest temperature possible, called **absolute zero**. On the kelvin scale absolute zero is at −273 °C. 0 °C is the same as 273 K.

> Note that we don't write in the ° (degree) sign on the kelvin scale; we just use a K to show that the kelvin scale is being used.

Here is a comparison of the three temperature scales:

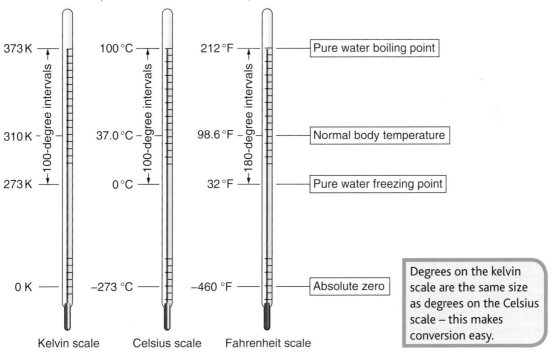

373 K ← 100-degree intervals →	100 °C ← 100-degree intervals →	212 °F ← 180-degree intervals →	Pure water boiling point
310 K	37.0 °C	98.6 °F	Normal body temperature
273 K	0 °C	32 °F	Pure water freezing point
0 K	−273 °C	−460 °F	Absolute zero

Kelvin scale   Celsius scale   Fahrenheit scale

> Degrees on the kelvin scale are the same size as degrees on the Celsius scale – this makes conversion easy.

Go further

◯ Hot and cold: Measuring temperature

You should be familiar with the concept of measuring temperature and with the apparatus used to do this – a thermometer (if not, refer back to the 'Investigations in science' section on thermometers). Dipping your finger into a liquid, or touching a hot object, is not accurate or quantitative or safe!

Different thermometers

There are many different types of thermometer as well as the liquid-in-glass type discussed in the 'Investigations in science' section at the start of this book.

Thermocouples have two different wires twisted together. Two sets of these junctions are connected to an instrument (a galvanometer) that measures voltage. The thermocouple produces a voltage when it is heated. One of the junctions is put into melting ice at 0 °C to provide a reference point and the other junction is used to measure the temperature you want to know.

Thermocouples have several advantages:

- they can work at higher temperatures than many other types of thermometer
- they can be used to measure the temperature of very small objects.

Thermocouples can be built into **temperature probes**. These have a metal or glass casing outside the thermocouple, which means that they can be pushed into quite hard objects. Temperature probes are very useful for measuring the temperature of foods (such as meat and fish) and soil.

A cheap and convenient thermometer uses a **liquid crystal strip** that changes colour according to temperature. These strips are used as aquarium thermometers and can give a rapid indication of your skin temperature if placed against the forehead.

Thermometers can also be digital, such as room thermostats on your central heating system or medical thermometers placed in the mouth or underarm area. These devices contain an electronic sensor called a thermistor, which changes electric resistance (see Chapter 9) with a changing temperature.

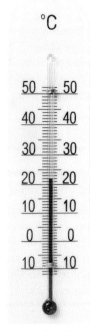

°C

■ An indoor liquid-in-glass thermometer

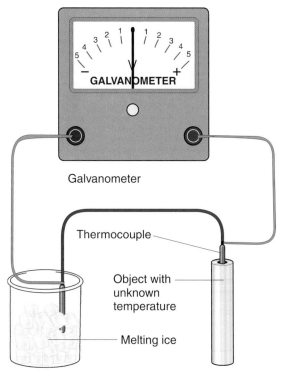

Galvanometer

Thermocouple

Object with unknown temperature

Melting ice

■ A thermocouple thermometer

Body temperature: How warm is warm blooded?

Humans, like other mammals, are **warm blooded**. This means that they can keep their body temperature constant even when the temperature of their surroundings is changing.

Normal human body temperature is 36.9 °C. We can check just how warm a human is by using a thermometer. Doctors can use a special thermometer with a very short scale that starts at the lowest possible body temperature someone can have and goes up to the highest. Many people have a thermometer like this at home. If you aren't feeling very well, your mother or father can check your temperature.

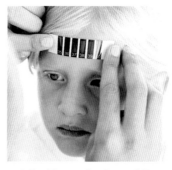

■ A liquid crystal strip used for measuring body temperature

Did you know?

The human body temperature can be measured with a liquid-in-glass thermometer, either:

- under the tongue
- or in the armpit.

The thermometer should be left in place for the recommended time before reading it.

Did you know?

Our body temperature is normally about 37 °C. If micro-organisms infect our body, the temperature may go up to 39–40 °C. This is called a *fever*. If the temperature gets higher than this, it can be very dangerous. (Enzymes and other proteins, for example, do not work properly at higher temperatures.)

Linear scale (35 °C to 42 °C).

Marker at 36.9 °C to show normal body temperature.

Constriction holds liquid in place whilst reading the temperature.

Liquid

Thin wall of bulb (so thermal energy is conducted very quickly to liquid)

■ Measuring body temperature

In summary: Energy and temperature

- Temperature is a way of describing how hot or cold an object is. It gives a measure of how concentrated the thermal (internal) energy is in an object. The unit of temperature most commonly used in your science studies is the degree Celsius (°C), and temperature is measured using a thermometer.
- Thermal (internal) energy is one form of energy. The unit of energy is called a joule (J).

An object can contain a great deal of thermal (internal) energy without having a high temperature. For example, a warm bath contains a great deal of thermal energy, but it is not very hot. This is because the thermal energy is spread out between the many particles of water in the bath. An object may contain a lot of other types of energy without being warm. Foods and fuels contain a great deal of energy, but they don't become hot until the energy is released as thermal energy when the object burns.

Temperature and the kinetic theory

You will learn in your chemistry studies that the **particle theory** explains the behaviour of solids, liquids and gases in terms of moving particles (see Chemistry, Chapter 1). When the particles are close together, there are strong forces between them and they attract one another. When a substance is heated, the particles move more quickly (and so tend to spread out by diffusion if the substance is a liquid or gas). The source energy is transferred to the particles as increased **kinetic energy**. At the same time the substance's temperature goes up.

The **temperature** of a substance is a measure of the **average kinetic energy of its particles**.

Exercise 1.2: Temperature

1 (a) What is the melting point of pure water using the Celsius scale?

   (b) What is the boiling point of pure water using the Celsius scale?

2 What is the body temperature of a normal healthy human?

3 Explain how a thermometer works.

4 Sugar and fat contain a lot of energy. Ice cream contains a lot of sugar and fat. Why isn't ice cream hot?

5 Which is hotter, a burning sparkler or the school swimming pool? Which one has the most thermal energy?

Extension question

6 Two liquids often used in thermometers are mercury and alcohol. Some of the properties of these two liquids are compared in this table:

	Mercury	Alcohol
Boiling point	365 °C	78.5 °C
Freezing point	−39 °C	−117 °C
Colour	Silver	Clear, but can be dyed
Cost	Expensive	Cheap
Conducts thermal energy	Well (heats up quickly)	Not so well (heats up slowly)
Toxicity	Poisonous	Not poisonous in small amounts
Metal or not	Metal	Non-metal
Conducts electricity	Well	An insulator
Flammability	Non-flammable	Flammable
Density	High	Low
Surface tension	High	Not so high
Degree of expansion when heated	Average	Large

(a) Which property is most important if you want a very sensitive thermometer?

(b) Why is alcohol most common in school laboratory thermometers?

(c) Which type of thermometer would be most useful for measuring the temperature of a lamb stew?

(d) Which liquid would be best-suited in a thermometer used to measure the temperature in a freezer?

Thermal energy: Insulators and conductors

Materials that allow thermal energy to pass through them are called thermal conductors. Some materials are better thermal conductors than others. A good thermal conductor often feels cold because it's so good at conducting thermal energy away from your hand (assuming it's colder than your hand in the first place).

Some materials do not let thermal energy pass through them. These materials are called thermal insulators. Being a thermal insulator is very useful in helping to stop thermal energy moving from one place to another. For example, think of oven gloves, a plastic handle on a saucepan, a cork teapot stand, the plastic casing of a refrigerator, and a tea cosy.

We can help reduce thermal energy loss from our homes by having good insulation, such as loft insulation, cavity wall insulation and double-glazed windows.

Conduction

We can use the idea of kinetic energy in particles (particle theory) to explain what happens when a hot object is placed in **contact** with a cold object.

Metals are good conductors of thermal energy because of the way in which their atoms are packed together. If one end of a bar of metal is heated, the atoms at that end will start to vibrate because of the thermal energy. These atoms will pass on their vibration to other atoms near them.

In this way thermal energy is passed along the metal, as shown below:

Thermal energy moves from higher temperature to lower temperature.

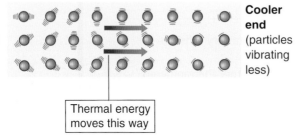

Hotter end (particles vibrating more)

Cooler end (particles vibrating less)

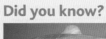

Thermal energy moves this way

■ Thermal energy transfer by conduction

Here is a summary of some good conductors and some poor ones:

Good conductors	Poor conductors (insulators)
Metals – especially silver, copper and aluminium	Glass
	Water
	Plastic
	Wood
	Materials with air trapped in them – wool, fibrewool, fur, feathers, plastic foam
	Air

Insulators such as those listed in the table above do not have this kind of structure. The particles in glass, plastic, rubber and wood cannot pass on this kinetic energy from one to another. Air is an excellent insulator because the particles are so far apart that they cannot easily pass on energy.

Did you know?

Sea mammals, like whales and dolphins, have a thick layer of blubber (fat) beneath the skin. This reduces the loss of thermal energy from the body to the cold water.

Conservation of energy

In this chapter you have learned that energy in all energy chains ends up as thermal (internal) energy. Energy is not lost during an energy transfer, but it can be changed from one form to another.

Power stations generate electricity by using some sort of fuel (more information in Chapter 2). Power stations are not 100 per cent efficient. In fact, about half of the energy in the fuel does not end up as electricity that we can use. This energy is wasted as far as we are concerned, but it has not disappeared. We say that this energy has been dissipated – the total energy is conserved, but in doing work energy is always spread out and so becomes less useful.

Another example of wasteful energy transfers is in the use of electrical appliances. Electrical appliances transfer all the energy supplied to them, but sometimes the energy is transformed into a form that isn't really useful to us. This energy will be wasted (unless we think of some very clever way of using it for something else!).

Most appliances release some energy as waste thermal energy. A computer or laptop has a fan inside it to get rid of the thermal energy – that's why it is so noisy.

A light bulb makes its surroundings warmer as well as lighter. It transfers thermal energy ∿∿∿ as well as light energy ———— to its surroundings.

Energy input → **Useful device** → **Useful energy output**

This can be used to carry out **work** that is useful to humans.

Wasted energy: Thermal and sound ↓

This energy is **dissipated.**

If we measure how much energy we put into a device and how much energy we get out of the device, we can work out how efficient the device is. Efficiency of a device or machine compares the energy used by the device with the useful energy given out by the device.

$$\text{Efficiency} = \frac{\text{useful energy OUTPUT}}{\text{energy INPUT}} \times 100$$

This diagram shows the efficiency of a common power tool, an electric drill:

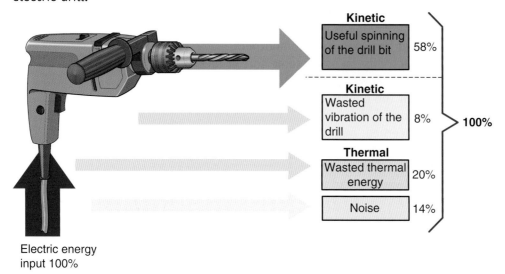

Electric energy
input 100%

Remember, the Law of Conservation of Energy states that:

Total energy output = energy input

We can use a special type of diagram to look at the energy transformations and losses when using a machine. This is called a Sankey diagram.

A Sankey diagram for the electric drill is shown below:

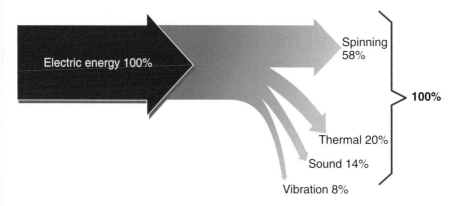

An important example of energy transformation occurs in the engine of a car. We use cars a great deal in the UK and it is important to realise how much of the stored energy in a fossil fuel (petrol) is wasted.

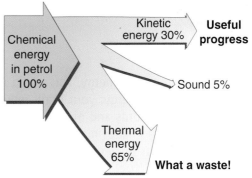

The Law of Conservation of Energy

You have learned about the Law of Conservation of Energy. When energy is dissipated we can't use it any more but, as we have just learned, it has not been lost. What in fact has happened is that the energy has been changed into some other form.

Energy can never be created nor destroyed – this is the **Law of Conservation of Energy**.

A final point to remember is that the conservation of energy is *not* the same as *saving energy*, which you will learn about in Chapter 2.

Exercise 1.3: Energy conservation

1 What forms of energy does a television set produce?

2 Give one reason why you should never put a piece of paper over a lamp to cut down the light it gives out.

2 Energy resources

Everything you do requires energy. You would not be able to read this book without energy; your brain requires energy to form images of the words and pictures on a page and to understand what these images mean. Where does this energy come from? Your body uses **food** as a source of energy. The food is the 'fuel' that supplies the energy for the processes of life.

Fuels and energy resources

Cities and towns also need large amounts of energy. Heating, lighting, transport and industry all require energy.

Fossil fuels

Much of the energy for running cities comes from fossil fuels: coal, gas and oil. The thermal energy produced by burning fossil fuels is used to boil water and the steam drives turbines that generate electricity.

Fossil fuels took millions of years to form (more information is given in the next section of this chapter) and we are using them up much more quickly than that. These are called non-renewable resources. We need to conserve fuels by reducing the amount of energy that we use.

Renewable energy resources

In some parts of the world, **water** can be used to generate energy, for example by harnessing tides and waves to drive turbines and generate electricity – this is called **tidal power.**

Electricity can also be generated by rivers in mountainous countries. Rivers are dammed to form large lakes and water is then allowed to flow down steadily through large turbines. This is called **hydroelectric power** and is a well-established source that contributes to world energy production at a level around 15 per cent.

Other energy sources are **solar power** in sunny regions and **wind power** in windy areas. If you go to Cornwall, for example, you will see many wind turbines perched on top of hills, turning in the wind.

Water power, wind power and solar power are all renewable energy resources because they can be replaced naturally and so will not run out.

Of all the renewable energy resources, hydroelectric power contributes the most global energy but still produces much less than coal, oil or nuclear (see below), all of which contribute large amounts to world energy production. The renewables contribute much lower amounts of energy, are currently costly or unreliable, or are only available in particular places on a small scale.

Go further

Nuclear power

Another source of energy we must consider is the energy produced by splitting atoms (for atoms, see Chemistry, Chapter 1). This breaking up of atoms can be made to happen very rapidly, with a great release of energy. This energy source is called nuclear power. The thermal energy produced in nuclear reactors can be used to boil water and to drive a turbine that generates electricity, just as in coal and power stations.

Energy supplies

We can get the energy we need in many different ways. However, the information we have on existing and projected energy supplies from the traditional energy sources (coal, oil and natural gas) indicates that they will increasingly be unable to satisfy our energy needs. Unless renewable energy sources are developed, there is the likelihood of a serious energy shortage in the not-so-distant future.

One of the challenges we face is how to choose which energy sources will give the energy the world needs as reliably, safely and cheaply as possible, with the least harm to the environment.

This is the basis of the **world energy crisis.**

The table below summarises some of the issues associated with a variety of energy sources:

Source	Advantages	Disadvantages	Lifetime
Wood	Easy to find	Limited amount Destruction of rainforests	Unlimited (providing forests are responsibly managed)
Biomass (see later in chapter)	Easy to do	Uneconomic	Unlimited
Fossil fuels Coal Oil Gas	 Many deposits Easy to extract Easy to extract	 Pollution Pollution Pollution	 Approx. 120 years* Approx. 60 years* Approx. 60 years*
Renewable Hydro	 Uses naturally occurring valleys in mountainous regions to channel water	 Limited number of rivers Destructive to environment when valleys are flooded	 Unlimited
Wind	Large amounts of energy	Expensive to concentrate Wind does not always blow Unsightly additions to landscape Wind farms take up large areas of land	Unlimited
Solar	Large amounts of energy but it is not always sunny Solar power is more economical in sunnier countries	Expensive to concentrate Sun does not shine all the time	Unlimited
Wave	Large amounts of energy	Expensive to concentrate Damage to environment	Unlimited
Nuclear	Non-polluting in use	Radioactive waste	Unlimited

* These figures are based on the lifetime of current global reserves and do not account for the discovery of new reserves or new extraction technologies being developed. These technologies can be extremely controversial ('fracking', for example).

You may be wondering what we mean by 'expensive to concentrate'? Well, quite simply, concentration is a measure of how spread out the energy is. The more spread out it is, the more it costs to gather it together to create a usable quantity of electricity. For example, there is enough energy in the air of a room to boil a kettle, but how would you trap it and turn it into electricity?

In the case of wind and solar sources, the energy is spread out over a large area and so it **costs a lot** to put it in a concentrated form that can be used. In the case of coal, oil and gas, the energy is very concentrated and in the case of nuclear even more so. If energy is not concentrated, you cannot use it. So, the extent to which a fuel is concentrated plays a very important part in helping us to decide which source will provide the most reliable, safe and cheap energy, with the least harm to the environment in the future.

Exercise 2.1: Energy resources

1 Complete the following paragraphs. Use words from this list, you may not need to use them all.

Bunsen	thermal	renewable	natural gas
energy	fossil	oxygen	potential

(a) A fuel is a store of _____ that can be released by burning in air. The air supplies the gas _____ required for the burning process. Burning a candle shows that _____ energy and light energy are given out during the burning process. In the laboratory a _____ burner can give a controllable supply of thermal energy by the burning of _____ .

(b) Coal and gas are examples of _____ fuels – once they are burned, they cannot be replaced. Water and wind power are _____ energy resources because they can be naturally replaced and so will not run out.

Extension questions

2 This table shows how energy is being used in the United Kingdom (2010):

Use of energy	Percentage of total energy used
Industry	29
Domestic (in homes)	31
Transport	26
Other uses	

(a) Work out the percentage of energy used for other purposes.
(b) Plot a bar chart of these figures.
(c) Give two uses of energy that might be in the 'other uses' category.
(d) Make a list of five different ways we use energy in the home.

3 This table shows the sources of energy generated in the United Kingdom in 2010:

Source	Percentage of total energy
Oil	1.5
Natural gas	38.5
Coal	30.0
Nuclear	26.3
Water	1.5
Others	

(a) Work out the percentage of 'other' sources of energy.
(b) What is the most likely source of energy in the 'other' category?
(c) Make a pie chart of this information.
(d) Give two reasons why we should use less coal and oil.
(e) Give one reason why we *should* use more nuclear power, and one reason why we are *anxious* about using nuclear power.

Working Scientifically

More about fossil fuels

Coal, oil and natural gas are called **fossil fuels** because they were formed millions of years ago. These fuels are the remains of organic material, such as the bodies of dead animals and plants that have not been allowed to decompose for one reason or another.

Fossil fuels store **chemical energy** that can be released as other forms of energy, such as thermal and light, when the fuels are burned. Because fossil fuels take so long to form and cannot be remade from the products of burning, they are known as **non-renewable** (sometimes called **capital**) **resources**. We cannot replace them, so they will eventually run out.

Fossil fuels are common energy resources

Coal is used for heating homes (not so much nowadays) and in power stations for generating electricity.

Petrol and **diesel** are made from oil. They are used as fuel for cars, lorries, ships and boats. More and more engines use diesel because it is more economical.

Natural gas is mainly methane. It is used for heating and cooking in homes and factories, and in power stations for generating electricity.

FUEL + OXYGEN

⬇

CARBON DIOXIDE + WATER
+

⬇

ENERGY

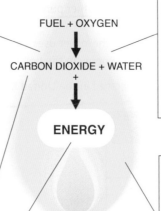

Kerosene (paraffin) is a cheap fuel made from oil. It is used domestically for heating, and industrially as fuel for aircraft.

There may be other wastes, such as ash and sulfur dioxide.

There will be light, thermal and perhaps some kinetic energy.

Butane and **propane** are used in camping and caravan stoves for cooking and in home gas heaters. It is pressurised for storage as liquid, and can be used as LPG (Liquefied Petroleum Gas) in cars and vans.

The formation of fossil fuels

Plants use sunlight energy to store chemical energy in the molecules that make up their bodies, via the process of photosynthesis (see Biology, Chapter 7).

Millions of years ago some of these plants would have been eaten by small animals, and some of them would have died before they were eaten. Dead animals and plants are usually quickly decomposed by the action of fungi and bacteria, but conditions in the environment might make this happen more slowly. It is the chemical energy in the bodies of these long-dead and partly decomposed animals and plants that is released when we burn fossil fuels. Look at the diagrams below to see how fossil fuels are formed.

Stages in the formation of coal: Fossil fuel from trees

Tree ferns lived 300 million years ago. As they died, they fell down and began to rot. The decay was very slow and the rotting plants formed a thick layer on the wet and swampy floor of the forest.

Bacteria changed the decaying plants to *peat*. This can be used as a fuel.

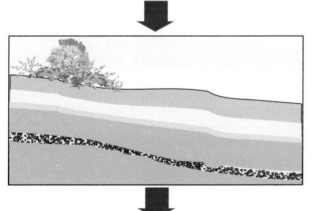

The land sank and layers of mud and rock were laid over the peat. As more and more rocks were laid down, the peat was exposed to **greater pressure and higher temperature.**

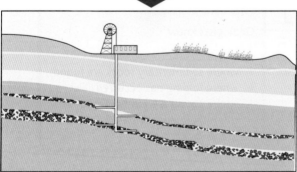

Over millions of years the layers turned into hard coal. The coal is collected by digging pits and mines.

> **Did you know?**
> Because decay is slow, coal often contains fossils of plants from 300 million years ago. The period when coal was formed is called the **Carboniferous Period.**

Formation of oil and natural gas: Fossil fuels from the sea

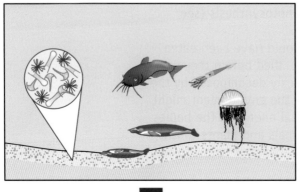

Microscopic plants and animals have trapped chemical energy in their bodies.

When these organisms die, their bodies sink to the bottom of the sea.

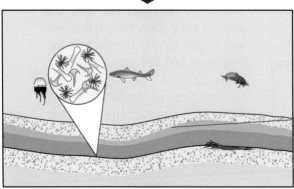

The bodies are covered by layers of mud and sand. As the bodies decay, they are changed to thick black **crude oil** by **high temperatures and pressures.**

The sedimentary rocks laid down in the sea are porous. The tiny holes allow liquids to move slowly through the rock.

Drilling rigs tap off the gas and oil.

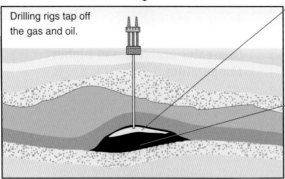

Some decay continues and provides gas (mainly methane). This is less dense than the oil and so collects on the top of the oil.

As the rock layers fold, crude oil becomes trapped under solid, hard rock. Pockets of trapped oil collect.

Did you know?
Geologists know:

- where to drill for oil
- where sedimentary rocks are found
- where folding has occurred
- where sound wave reflection tells them there are cavities or chambers in the rock.

Fracking

Hydraulic fracturing, or **fracking**, is a technique designed to recover gas and oil from shale rock. It is the process of drilling down into the earth before a high-pressure water mixture is directed at the rock to release the gas inside. Water, sand and chemicals are injected into the rock at high pressure, which allows the gas to flow out to the head of the well.

The process is carried out vertically or, more commonly, by drilling horizontally to the rock layer. The process can create new pathways to release gas or can be used to extend existing channels.

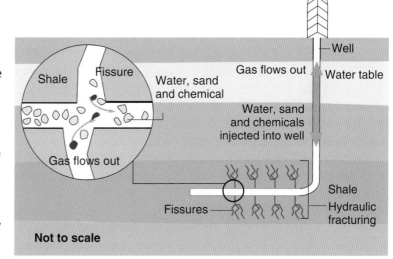

Not to scale

■ Shale gas extraction

Fracking can provide additional fuel for energy generation.

Fracking is controversial

Fracking has been widely used in the USA, where it has dramatically lowered energy prices and reduced dependence on imported sources of energy. However, it has prompted environmental concerns:

- Fracking uses huge amounts of water that must be transported to the fracking site, at significant environmental cost in air pollution and road congestion.
- Chemicals used in the process may escape and contaminate groundwater around the fracking site. Among the pollution concerns is the potential that these chemicals might cause cancer.
- The fracking process can cause small earth tremors. Two small earthquakes of 1.5 and 2.2 magnitude hit the Blackpool area in 2011 following fracking.
- Finally, environmental campaigners say that fracking is simply stopping energy companies and governments from investing in renewable sources of energy, and so is encouraging continued use of fossil fuels.

Where is fracking taking place?

Reserves of shale gas have been identified across swathes of the UK, particularly in the north of England. Test drilling has taken place, although demonstrators often disrupt this process. However, no commercial fracking has taken place yet, and drilling firms must apply for a fracking licence if they wish to continue with exploration.

Using fossil fuels

Wood (not a fossil fuel) was the first fuel to be used by humans from the time they first discovered fire. But from the nineteenth century onwards, humans began to use fossil fuels extensively. Coal was the easiest to extract from the Earth, and so this was the first fossil fuel to be widely used.

Oil and gas were not produced or used much until the twentieth century. By the end of the twentieth century oil and gas were more commonly used than coal. Oil can be used to make petrol and diesel fuel for motor vehicles, and to make many of the molecules needed for synthetic materials, such as plastics and fabrics.

> You will learn about burning (combustion) in Chemistry, Chapter 7.

All fossil fuels make carbon dioxide when they are burned, but coal is dirtier than gas and oil because it makes a lot of ash and smoke.

Different fuels for different uses

A fuel is a source of energy, so we might think that the most important thing about a fuel is the amount of energy it gives out when it is burned. This is important but it is not the only thing to consider. Other important factors are:

- Can the fuel be stored?
- Can the fuel be transported?
- Is the fuel easy to extract from the Earth?
- Is the fuel clean to use?
- Is the fuel solid, liquid or gas?
- Is it easy to ignite the fuel (to start it burning)?
- How much does it cost to extract the energy from the fuel?

Some fuels are better than others for a particular job. For example, petrol is a better fuel for cars than coal; you can deliver it through a hose from a petrol pump, and it is easier to ignite. Gas is a good fuel for camping stoves because it can be compressed into lightweight gas bottles that are easy and safe to carry.

Fossil fuels and electricity

Electricity is not a fuel, but most of it is produced by burning fossil fuels. These fuels are reliable, concentrated forms of energy, but need to be transported from where they are extracted to where they are burned in the power stations. You will see more of this later in this chapter, but let's just summarise some of the advantages and disadvantages of generating electricity from these different fossil fuels:

Fossil fuel	Advantages	Disadvantages
Coal	Still large deposits of this fuel available, enough for the next 200–300 years approximately	Extraction and burning makes pollution
Natural gas	Burns with less pollution than coal or oil	Difficult to find
Oil	Can easily be transported in pipelines	Oil spills are very harmful to wildlife

Conservation of fuel reserves

It is important that we save fossil fuels because:

- they are **non-renewable** and are running out
- burning them is the main cause of **air pollution**.

Fuels can be conserved by:

- increasing the use of alternative, renewable energy sources (see later in this chapter) and nuclear power
- using more efficient machines
- being more careful with the use of energy; reducing energy wastage, for example insulating your home.

Exercise 2.2: Fossil fuels

1 Which of the following is the best definition of a fossil fuel?
   (a) Something that can be burned to give off heat.
   (b) Remains of animals and plants that store energy.
   (c) Remains of long-dead animals and plants that act as a store of energy.
   (d) A store of energy that can go through a reaction to release the energy.

2 Here are some statements about coal. Sort them out to tell the story of the formation of coal:
   - The rivers washed sediment on top.
   - The material was heated under pressure for millions of years.
   - Coal is a store of chemical energy.
   - When trees died, they fell into swamps but did not decompose.
   - The Sun shone on the Earth, and the trees absorbed light energy from the Sun.
   - More trees fell on top.
   - 300 million years ago there were huge forests of simple, fern-like trees.

3 Here are some statements about oil and natural gas. Sort them into the correct order to tell the story of the formation of these fuels:
   - People build oil platforms to drill for oil.
   - Thermal energy and pressure changed the material in the bodies of plants and animals into oil.
   - The small organisms died.
   - The plants were eaten by small animals in the sea.
   - The Sun shone on the Earth and tiny plants in the sea obtained their energy from the Sun.
   - Movements of the Earth compressed the remains of the small organisms.
   - Gas pipelines bring gas to homes and factories.
   - Sediment piled up on the bodies.
   - Conditions change, so that some bodies are allowed to decay.
   - Gas is collected from above the oil wells.
   - Over millions of years, gas given off from the decay processes is trapped.
   - When the seas dried up, the small organisms became trapped.

4 What are the two reasons why it is important to conserve fuels?

5 In Norway, wood is a very popular fuel. Wood only gives out 10 kJ of energy per gram of fuel burned, but oil gives out 46 kJ of energy per gram. Suggest a reason why wood is so popular as a fuel in Norway.

Renewable energy resources

What does 'renewable' mean?

Renewable energy sources do not get smaller as they are used. For example, collecting energy from the wind does not change the amount of wind energy that will be available in the future. Renewable energy resources are sometimes called **alternative** energy resources, because they are seen as an alternative to the use of fossil fuels.

There are some important points to remember about renewable energy resources:

- they are not used up
- they do not pollute the atmosphere.

  However, with the partial exception of hydropower:

- they are several times more expensive than fossil fuels
- they can be unreliable and available only in particular places on a small scale
- they contribute very little energy (except hydro)
- they can have bad environmental effects.

What types of renewable energy are available?

Whatever form of renewable energy is available, it must be converted into a form of energy that we can use. Most of our machines and appliances work on electrical energy, so a renewable energy source must be capable of conversion into electricity (with the exception of solar panels, which enable the Sun to heat the water directly, and water from hot springs and geysers).

Electricity is generated using a **turbine** and a generator, as shown below.

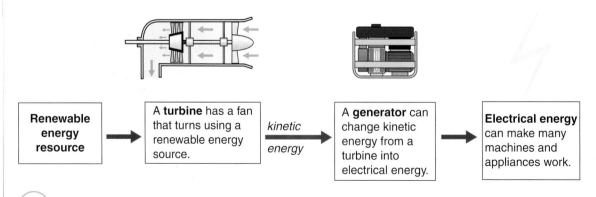

| Renewable energy resource | → | A **turbine** has a fan that turns using a renewable energy source. | *kinetic energy* | A **generator** can change kinetic energy from a turbine into electrical energy. | → | **Electrical energy** can make many machines and appliances work. |

There are several different forms of renewable energy. Engineers tend to use the one that is most easily available – this can be very different from one country to another. For example, **hydroelectric power** is available only in mountainous areas with swift-flowing rivers (Scotland, for example) and geothermal **power** (electric power generated using very hot water or steam that breaks through the Earth's surface from the hot interior) is only available in areas with hot springs and geysers (Iceland, for example).

Here are some alternative sources of renewable energy made available to us through the skill of engineers:

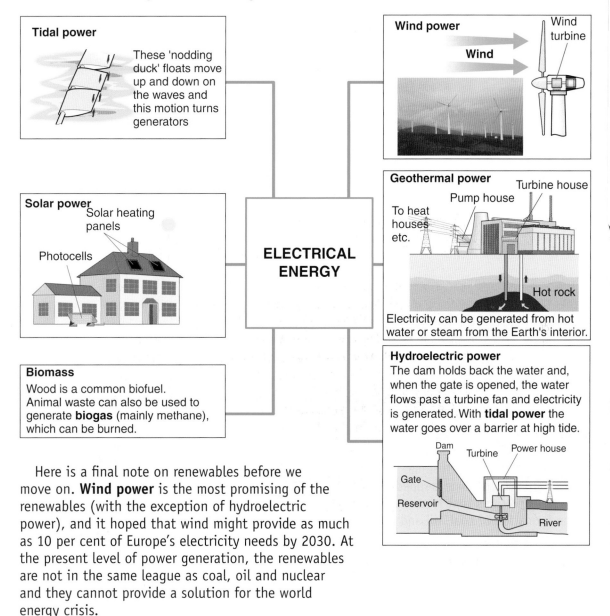

Tidal power

These 'nodding duck' floats move up and down on the waves and this motion turns generators

Wind power

Wind turbine

Wind

Solar power

Solar heating panels

Photocells

ELECTRICAL ENERGY

Geothermal power

Turbine house

Pump house

To heat houses etc.

Hot rock

Electricity can be generated from hot water or steam from the Earth's interior.

Biomass

Wood is a common biofuel. Animal waste can also be used to generate **biogas** (mainly methane), which can be burned.

Hydroelectric power

The dam holds back the water and, when the gate is opened, the water flows past a turbine fan and electricity is generated. With **tidal power** the water goes over a barrier at high tide.

Dam

Turbine

Power house

Gate

Reservoir

River

Here is a final note on renewables before we move on. **Wind power** is the most promising of the renewables (with the exception of hydroelectric power), and it hoped that wind might provide as much as 10 per cent of Europe's electricity needs by 2030. At the present level of power generation, the renewables are not in the same league as coal, oil and nuclear and they cannot provide a solution for the world energy crisis.

Energy from the Sun

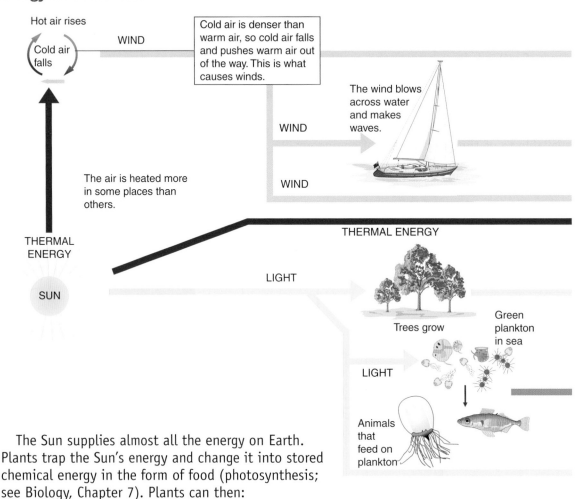

Hot air rises

Cold air falls

WIND

Cold air is denser than warm air, so cold air falls and pushes warm air out of the way. This is what causes winds.

The wind blows across water and makes waves.

WIND

WIND

The air is heated more in some places than others.

THERMAL ENERGY

THERMAL ENERGY

LIGHT

SUN

Trees grow

Green plankton in sea

LIGHT

Animals that feed on plankton

The Sun supplies almost all the energy on Earth. Plants trap the Sun's energy and change it into stored chemical energy in the form of food (photosynthesis; see Biology, Chapter 7). Plants can then:

- use the food themselves
- be eaten by animals and so pass on the chemical energy to the animals
- die and pass on the chemical energy to bacteria and fungi
- die and, together with some dead animals, become trapped under conditions that favour the formation of coal, oil and natural gas.

The part that the Sun plays in the supply of our energy resources is shown above.

Energy sources that don't depend on the Sun	
Tides (Mainly caused by the Moon's gravity – see Chapter 3)	Water is trapped behind a dam on a tidal river when the tide comes in (twice each day). The flow of trapped water can be used to generate electricity.
Geothermal	The breakdown of radioactive substances inside the Earth produces heat. The heat can be used to warm water, and the water can heat homes and factories.
Nuclear fuel (e.g. uranium)	Uranium can be mined from close to the Earth's surface. Electricity is generated from the energy released by splitting atoms in nuclear reactors.

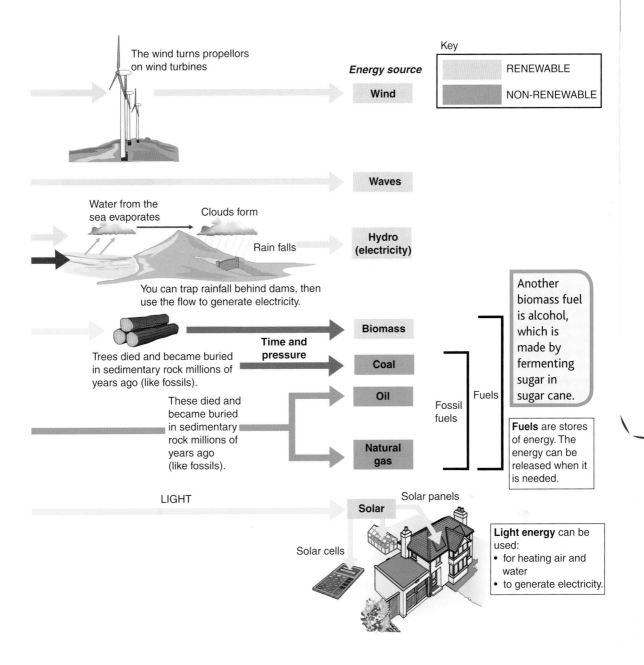

The wind turns propellors on wind turbines

Energy source

Wind

Waves

Water from the sea evaporates

Clouds form

Rain falls

Hydro (electricity)

You can trap rainfall behind dams, then use the flow to generate electricity.

Biomass

Time and pressure

Trees died and became buried in sedimentary rock millions of years ago (like fossils).

Coal

These died and became buried in sedimentary rock millions of years ago (like fossils).

Oil

Natural gas

Fossil fuels

Fuels

Another biomass fuel is alcohol, which is made by fermenting sugar in sugar cane.

Fuels are stores of energy. The energy can be released when it is needed.

LIGHT

Solar panels

Solar

Solar cells

Light energy can be used:
• for heating air and water
• to generate electricity.

Solar power

All fossil fuels originally made their stored chemical energy from the sunlight energy trapped by photosynthesis (see Biology, Chapter 7). Energy direct from the Sun is a very attractive energy source because there is no foreseeable reduction in the amount of the Sun's energy landing on the Earth. Having said that, though, it is important to remember that solar power is expensive because the Sun's energy is spread very thinly over the Earth's surface, so we have to go to a lot of trouble to concentrate it.

The simplest way to make direct use of the Sun's thermal energy is to put solar panels on roofs of buildings and let the Sun's rays directly heat the water running through the panels. Some solar cells change light and thermal energy from the Sun into an electrical current, for example, on a calculator; these are also extremely useful for equipment that is a long way away from a generator, such as a space station.

Investigation: What factors affect the performance of solar panels?

Solar panels are designed to collect as much of the Sun's energy as possible. Several factors affect how well a solar panel absorbs solar energy. These factors are investigated here, using water balloons as a model:

Step 1

- Each of the balloons contains the same volume of water, at the same temperature.
- Both balloons are the same colour.

Step 2

- The balloons are then covered with cloth.
- The hot lamp is kept at the same distance from the balloons.
- The temperature of the water is measured at the same time for the two balloons.

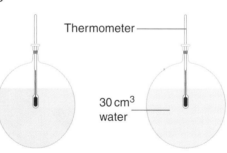

Thermometer

30 cm³ water

Black cloth   White cloth

Remember what makes a FAIR TEST!

- Change one variable (independent or input variable).
- Measure a second variable (dependent or outcome variable).
- Keep all other variables constant.

> The temperature can be measured with an electronic sensor and a datalogger.

1 This table shows some results obtained from this investigation.

Time, in minutes	Temperature, in °C	
	Black cloth	White cloth
0	16	16
4	20	19
8	25	23
12	29	26
16	33	30
20	37	32

(a) Which balloon would you expect to have the warmer water after 15 minutes?

(b) Which colour would you suggest should be used for a solar panel?

(c) Why is it important to use the same volume of water in each balloon?

(d) Describe how you could use the same apparatus to find out whether a shiny or a dull surface is better for a solar panel.

Exercise 2.3: Renewable energy resources

1 Match the type of renewable energy with its feature:

Renewable energy resource	Features of this resource
Solar energy	Water current turns a turbine
Geothermal energy	Can heat water or generate electricity
Wind	Sea water turns a turbine
Tides and waves	Thermal energy from underground rocks
Hydroelectric power	Material from the growth of plants
Biomass	Can move small boats or turn wind turbines

2 Why do we describe electricity as the most useful form of energy?

3 This table lists the percentage contribution of each resource to all renewable energy resources:

◼ Energy consumption outlook in Western Word 1990 (World Energy Needs and Resources)

Energy resource	Percentage contribution
Hydroelectric	77.4
Biomass	18.6
Geothermal	1.9
Solar heating	1.9
Wind	0.2

(a) Make a pie chart of this information.
(b) Which renewable resource is most useful in a forested part of the world?
(c) Suggest why geothermal energy makes such a small contribution.

4 Explain what is meant by a 'renewable' form of energy.

Electricity

As you have learned, fuels and renewable energy sources can release energy in various forms. The most useful form of energy for human activities however, is **electricity**.

Getting an electricity supply

Large appliances often use electricity from the mains, usually through a socket in the wall. Because the mains electricity is delivered from a wall socket, it means that these appliances can't be moved very far.

Smaller electrical appliances often use batteries to supply the energy. Batteries are devices that contain one or more electrochemical 'cells', which covert stored chemical energy into electrical energy (see Chapter 9 for more details).

Appliances that can run on batteries can be moved from place to place. Batteries can store electricity, but they eventually **run down**, which means they don't have enough electrical energy to run the appliance. Batteries need to be *replaced* by fresh batteries, or *recharged* so that their energy is replaced.

Go further

The passage of electricity: Conductors and insulators

As we know, electricity needs something to travel through, to get from the place where it is made to the place where it is used. Materials that allow electricity to pass through them are called conductors because they can **conduct** electricity.

The materials that are used most frequently as conductors are metals, such as copper in wiring. Some non-metals, such as graphite, which is a form of carbon, are also used. There are other conductors but they are not so easy to use. Tap or sea water, for example, is not so easy to control and use, but can be a very good conductor, which is why it is so dangerous to be near a source of electricity in wet conditions. (Pure water does not conduct electricity.)

Materials that do not conduct electricity are called insulators. Non-metallic substances are usually good insulators. Plastic, rubber, glass and wood are good examples, but you should not let them get wet.

> You have to be careful not to touch overhead power lines with carbon fibre (graphite) fishing rods or kites, particularly with wet strings, because they can conduct electricity.

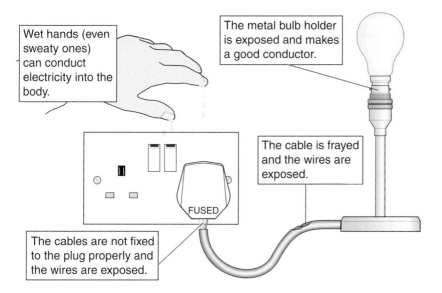

Wet hands (even sweaty ones) can conduct electricity into the body.

The metal bulb holder is exposed and makes a good conductor.

The cable is frayed and the wires are exposed.

FUSED

The cables are not fixed to the plug properly and the wires are exposed.

Dangerous electricity

Electricity is a very valuable form of energy, and most of us couldn't imagine our lives without it. However, it can also be very dangerous if it is not controlled. Electrical energy can cause great damage to our bodies and could even kill us, so it is very, very important to take great care when using electrical items.

NEVER:

- stick scissors, pens or anything else into a mains socket
- use electrical appliances near water
- touch switches or sockets with wet hands (use pull-cords for light switches in bathrooms).

ALWAYS:

- hold the plastic part of a plug when plugging in or unplugging appliances – it is insulated!

■ Electricity from batteries is less powerful than mains electricity, and when batteries run down they must be recharged at the mains. Rechargeable batteries can discharge quickly and can cause burns, particularly when they malfunction or are damaged.

Exercise 2.4: Energy and electricity

1 Which one of the following is **not** one of the rules for working safely with electricity?
   (a) Keep water away.
   (b) Don't stick anything into a power outlet.
   (c) Ensure cables are insulated.
   (d) Wear safety glasses.

2 Which of these sentences is the best description of a cell (battery) and what it does?
   (a) A small box for storing electricity.
   (b) A source of mains electricity.
   (c) A case containing chemicals to provide energy to move a current around a circuit.
   (d) A method for providing electricity to power a machine.

3 Complete these sentences by choosing the missing words from this list:

   plastic   brass   conduct   insulator   lead   electricity   graphite

   The case of a plug is made from _____ because it is a good _____ . The pins of the plug need to _____ electricity, so they are made of _____ . The covering on a _____ is made of plastic, so that it will not conduct _____ . Some electrical machines use _____ (a kind of carbon) to conduct electricity between different parts of the motor.

Extension question

4 Here is a drawing of an electrical circuit. If the circuit is completed (i.e. it is a complete ring) and electricity can flow, then the lamp will light up. Explain how the apparatus could be used to test whether a material was an insulator or a conductor.

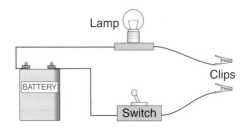

◯ Generating electricity from a fuel

You have learned that fuels can be used to release energy and the most useful form of energy for human activities is electricity. Here we will look at the process of generating electricity from fuels in more detail.

Power stations

Power stations are able to change the **chemical energy** of fuels into **electrical energy**. Most power stations burn **fossil fuels**. The fossil fuel is tipped into a large **furnace** and oxygen is then forced into the furnace. The burning fuel gives out a large amount of **thermal energy**. The thermal energy is then used to boil **water**, which turns into **steam**. The steam is forced along pipes to make powerful **jets** that hit the blades of a **turbine**. The turbine turns a shaft in the **generator** and **electricity** is made. This sequence is shown on the next page.

> Burning is a chemical reaction called combustion. See Chemistry, Chapter 7.

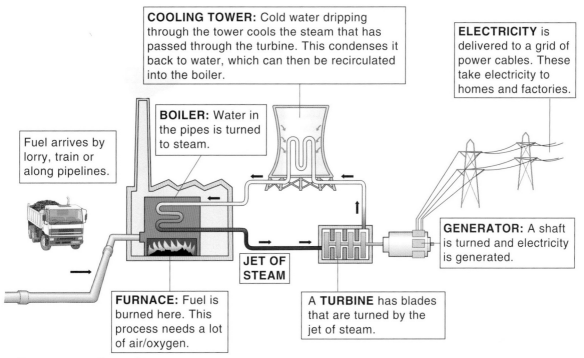

COOLING TOWER: Cold water dripping through the tower cools the steam that has passed through the turbine. This condenses it back to water, which can then be recirculated into the boiler.

ELECTRICITY is delivered to a grid of power cables. These take electricity to homes and factories.

BOILER: Water in the pipes is turned to steam.

Fuel arrives by lorry, train or along pipelines.

GENERATOR: A shaft is turned and electricity is generated.

JET OF STEAM

FURNACE: Fuel is burned here. This process needs a lot of air/oxygen.

A **TURBINE** has blades that are turned by the jet of steam.

How a power station works

The steam is still very hot after it hits the turbine and needs to be cooled so that it can be turned back into water before it is returned to the boiler. The steam is cooled in a cooling tower, where cold water is poured over the pipes that are carrying the steam. This cold water evaporates quickly. This is the steam we see coming from the cooling towers in power stations.

Go further

Efficiency of power stations

The efficiency of a power station describes how much energy is released from a certain mass of fuel. No power station is 100 per cent efficient and they always lose some of the energy from the fuel they are using. Some power stations are more efficient than others. Gas power stations are about 50 per cent efficient and are the most efficient of the main power station types we use.

Don't forget that fossil fuels are **non-renewable**, which means that eventually we will run out of them. The burning of fossil fuels also causes air pollution.

Making the most of electricity

Electricity that is generated in power stations must then be transferred to the homes and factories where it is needed. Most countries have a network of power cables leading from power stations to smaller substations and then on to homes and factories. These power cables are often carried overhead from power stations to the substation, hanging from tall pylons. The cables are usually then carried underground from the substations to homes.

Electricity is a very useful form of energy, because:

- It is easy to transfer along power lines and cables.
- It leaves no waste when it is used, so it is a clean form of energy.
- It is easily transformed into other forms of energy, such as the vibrations causing sound from a radio.
- It is easy to control electrical energy accurately. For example, think how fine the images can be from a digital camera.

There are one or two disadvantages when using electricity, however:

- It is not easy to store large amounts of electrical energy, so engineers have to balance carefully the production of electricity with its use.
- The transfer of electricity requires high voltages and these can be very dangerous.

Exercise 2.5: Generation of electricity

1 Why does a power station need cooling towers?

2 What is the difference between a turbine and a generator?

3 This table shows the percentage efficiency of different power stations:

Working Scientifically

Type of fuel used	Percentage efficiency
Coal	39
Gas	51
Oil	36
Nuclear	40

(a) Many coal-fuelled power stations are being converted to burn gas. Explain why this would be an advantage.

(b) Suggest two ways in which nuclear energy might be better than oil as a way of generating electricity.

(c) Why should we be reducing our use of all these fuels?

4 (a) Look at this diagram of a power station. Fill in the missing words in (i)–
    (v) to show how energy is lost as waste forms of energy.

Thermal energy losses at a power station

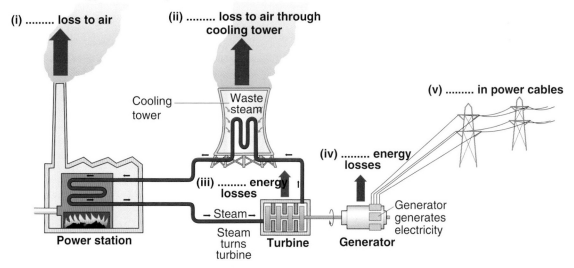

(i) .... loss to air

(ii) .... loss to air through cooling tower

(v) .... in power cables

Cooling tower

Waste steam

(iv) .... energy losses

(iii) .... energy losses

– Steam –

Steam turns turbine

Power station

Turbine

Generator

Generator generates electricity

(b) The Sankey diagram below shows the energy transfers and losses when
    energy generated in the power station is converted to light energy in
    your home.

Coal in power station 200 J

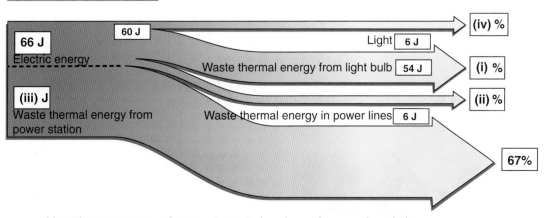

66 J
Electric energy

60 J

Light 6 J

(iv) %

Waste thermal energy from light bulb 54 J

(i) %

(iii) J
Waste thermal energy from power station

Waste thermal energy in power lines 6 J

(ii) %

67%

(i) What percentage of energy is wasted as thermal energy from light
     bulbs?
(ii) What percentage of energy is lost as waste thermal energy in the
     power lines?
(iii) How many joules of energy put into the power station end up as
     waste thermal energy from the power station itself?
(iv) What is the overall efficiency of the power station in converting
     energy to light in light bulbs?

Forces and linear motion

What is a force?

A **force** is either a **push** or a **pull**. You can't see a force, but you can see what a force does. Forces can change the:

- **speed** of things – they can make things speed up or slow down
- **direction** that something is moving in
- **shape** of things.

Forces act in one direction

We need to know two things about a force to understand what it is doing. We need to know: the **size** of the force and the **direction** in which the force is acting.

We use arrows to show the size and the direction of forces:

This arrow shows the force driving the motorbike forwards:
- the arrow is **long** because the force is big
- the arrow is pointing in the direction in which the engine is pushing the motorbike.

This arrow shows the force of air through which the motorbike is being driven:
- the arrow is **short** because the force is small
- the arrow is pointing at the motorbike because the force is **against the movement** of the motorbike.

This arrow shows the **resultant force**. This force is the difference between the bigger force and the smaller one. The length of the arrow tells you how big the force is and the direction tells you that the motorbike is moving forward.

When two different forces work on the same object, the **bigger** (longer arrow) **one 'wins'.**

Forces and motion

Things are moving all around us:

- On a very small scale, the particles that make up atoms and molecules are always moving (we say that they are in motion).
- Movement (motion) is more obvious in animals (including humans) and machines than the movement of particles.
- On an enormous scale, the Earth is in motion around the Sun, and the stars move around in the different galaxies.

Speed and movement

Speed tells us how fast an object is moving. The speed of any moving object is the distance it moves in a certain amount of time. The units we use for speed have to include **distance** and **time**. For example, we can describe speed in kilometres per hour (km/h), or in metres per second (m/s). The way that these units are written (i.e. a unit of distance divided by a unit of time) helps us with a definition of speed.

$$\text{Speed} = \frac{\text{distance}}{\text{time}}$$

We can write out this useful equation in symbols:

$$s = \frac{d}{t}$$

where: s = speed
d = distance
t = time taken

The prefixes to the names of units help you to work out their relative sizes.

e.g.   milli – means 'one thousandth': $\frac{1}{1000}$

centi – means 'one hundredth': $\frac{1}{100}$

kilo – means 'thousand': $1000 \times$

so   1 centimetre contains 10 millimetres

1 metre contains 100 centimetres
or 1000 millimetres

Measuring speed

If we are going to make an accurate measurement of speed, we need to know:

- the exact distance travelled (including the correct units)
- the exact length of time taken (including the correct units).

An example of a speed measurement that can be made in a school laboratory is shown in below.

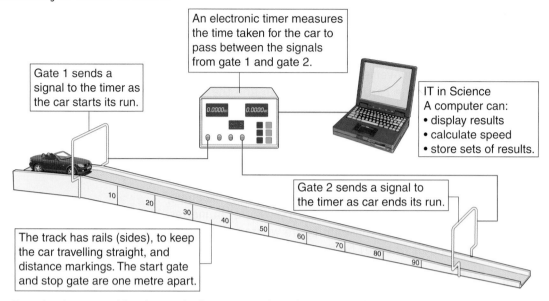

Gate 1 sends a signal to the timer as the car starts its run.

An electronic timer measures the time taken for the car to pass between the signals from gate 1 and gate 2.

IT in Science
A computer can:
• display results
• calculate speed
• store sets of results.

Gate 2 sends a signal to the timer as car ends its run.

The track has rails (sides), to keep the car travelling straight, and distance markings. The start gate and stop gate are one metre apart.

Exactly the same idea is used when measuring the speed of drag-racing cars or human athletes running a 100 m race.

Relative motion

If you travel in a car on the motorway, you may notice that other cars passing by *appear* to move slowly past you, even though you know the actual speeds of the two cars are very high. This is because of their relative motion to each other.

Another example of relative motion concerns two moving objects that are travelling in *opposite directions*. For example, a car may be travelling along a road running parallel to a railway line, and driving towards an oncoming train.

The method of calculation of relative speeds of two moving objects is summarised below:

Situation	Relative speed calculation
Objects moving in the same direction towards, or away from, each other (such as cars overtaking one another)	Fastest speed – slowest speed
Objects moving in opposite directions towards, or away from, each other (such as a car driving towards another car)	Speed of object A + speed of object B

Exercise 3.1: Forces

1 Choose words from this list to complete this paragraph about forces:

speed   size (magnitude)   direction   forces   shape

_____ are pushes or pulls, exerted by one thing on another. Forces can change the _____, _____ and direction of things. They have two important features: _____ and _____ . These two features of a force can be shown by drawing an arrow.

2 In the National Swimming Championships, the swimmers are timed electronically. A very accurate electronic clock is started as the starter's signal is given and stopped as the swimmers touch a pressure pad at the end of the pool. Work out the average speed for these race winners.

Event	Distance, in m	Time taken, in seconds	Speed, in m/s
Freestyle	50	28	
Backstroke	100	60	
Butterfly	100	56	
Breaststroke	200	140	
Individual medley	400	275	

3 **(a)** Two cars are travelling in the same direction on a road. The green car is travelling at 22 m/s in front of the silver car, which is travelling at 25 m/s. What is their relative speed?

(b) A railway line and a road are side by side. A train and a car are travelling in the same direction, with the train in front of the car. The train travels at 60 m/s and the car at 35 m/s. What is their relative speed?

(c) Mark Cavendish is a famous British cyclist. He is well known for his ability to sprint away from opponents at the end of a race.
The diagram shows the finish of a stage in the Tour de France. Mark Cavendish is sprinting at 68 km/hour and his nearest opponent can only manage 65 km/hour.

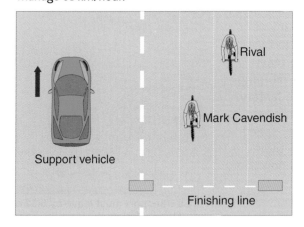

(i) What is their relative speed?

(ii) At the same time, the support vehicle for Mark Cavendish is returning to the area where all the cyclists gather after the race is finished. This vehicle is travelling at 35 km/hour – there is a lot of traffic on this road. What is the relative speed of Mark Cavendish and the driver in the support vehicle?

4 Anne wanted to investigate the speed of different model cars. She set up the same kind of apparatus as shown earlier in this chapter and obtained the following results:

Car number	Run 1, in seconds	Run 2, in seconds	Run 3, in seconds	Average time, in seconds
1	2.40	2.50	2.60	
2	2.90	2.75	2.78	
3	2.35	2.55	4.90	

(a) Which one of the results seems to be unreliable?

(b) Leaving out this result, work out the average speeds of the three cars and complete the table.

(c) What is the independent (input) variable in this experiment?

(d) What is the dependent (outcome) variable in this experiment?

(e) How could Anne be sure that this was a fair test?

Extension question

5 (a) Use the internet or a textbook to find:

    (i)   The speed of the fastest living organism.

    (ii) The speed of the fastest mammal on land.

    (iii) The world land speed record.

    (iv) The world water speed record.

In each case make sure that you include the correct units in your answer.

(b) The fastest a human has run (footspeed) on record is (at the time of writing) about 10.5 m/s by Usain Bolt, the Jamaican sprinter. He has held the world record for the 100 m sprint since 2009. His time was 9.58 seconds. How many times faster than this does the fastest mammal move on land?

Distance and time

Formula One racing teams need to travel around the world to take part in different grand prix. Many of these teams are based in England and need to take ferries to reach the European mainland. One team needed to be on a ferry by 10 o'clock in the morning and had to decide the best time to leave the factory base in Oxfordshire. Of course, a racing team would be well aware of the relationships between time, speed and distance. They could calculate how long their trip to the ferry terminal would take. This is how they worked things out:

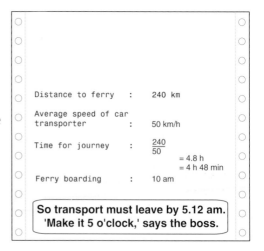

```
Distance to ferry      :     240 km

Average speed of car
transporter            :     50 km/h

Time for journey       :     240
                             ───
                             50
                                    = 4.8 h
                                    = 4 h 48 min

Ferry boarding         :     10 am
```

So transport must leave by 5.12 am. 'Make it 5 o'clock,' says the boss.

Speed triangle

Remember that **speed** is the **distance** travelled in a certain amount of **time** and there is an equation that relates these three measurements. If you know two of the things in the equation, you can always work out the other one. A 'speed triangle' can help you with this calculation.

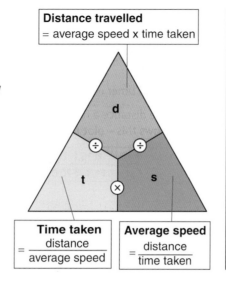

Distance travelled = average speed x time taken

Time taken = $\dfrac{\text{distance}}{\text{average speed}}$

Average speed = $\dfrac{\text{distance}}{\text{time taken}}$

Distance–time graphs

A distance–time graph is obtained if we plot how much distance is covered during a certain part of a journey. Here's an example. The graph below shows a boy's journey to school. He did not travel at a constant speed and we can use the graph to find out how fast he travelled at different stages of his journey:

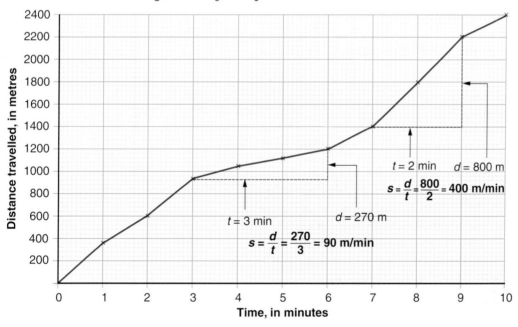

$t = 3$ min

$s = \dfrac{d}{t} = \dfrac{270}{3} = 90$ m/min

$d = 270$ m

$t = 2$ min $d = 800$ m

$s = \dfrac{d}{t} = \dfrac{800}{2} = 400$ m/min

Investigation: Reaction times

The aim of this experiment is to investigate reaction times of your classmates.

In pairs, you can make a simple reaction timer using a 30 cm ruler.

First, you need to understand that the distance a ruler falls depends on how long it has been falling. The table shows this – plot these data into a graph.

Time, in seconds	0	0.05	0.10	0.15	0.20	0.25	0.30
Distance fallen, in cm	0	1	5.0	11.3	20.0	31	45

To find your reaction time:

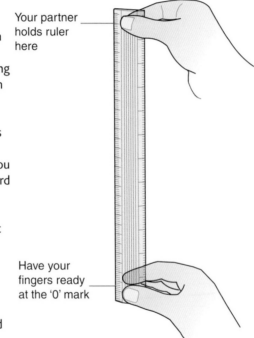

Your partner holds ruler here

Have your fingers ready at the '0' mark

- your partner should hold the ruler at the top end
- have your hand ready with your fingers at the 0 mark on the ruler, but not holding it, as shown in the diagram
- your partner should let go of the ruler and you should trap it as quickly as possible
- record the position that you trapped the ruler and record your results in a table like the one below
- repeat twice more, so that you have a total of three distances
- use the reaction time graph to work out how your 'distance fallen' measurements correspond to 'reaction times'.

Distance fallen, in cm	1	2	3	Average
Reaction time, in seconds				

Compare your results with other students in the class.

1 What is the range of values in the class?
2 Are boys 'faster' than girls?
3 Is your left hand 'faster' than your right hand?

Exercise 3.2: Distance and time

1 How far would you travel:
   (a) in 20 seconds if you ran at 5 m/s?
   (b) in 50 seconds if you were in an aeroplane travelling at 50 m/s?
   (c) in 90 minutes if you cycled at an average speed of 30 km/h?

2 How long will the following journeys take:
   (a) A 400 m walk at 2 m/s?
   (b) A 2 km run at 4 m/s?

3 Find the speed of:
   (a) a dog that runs 300 m in 12 s
   (b) a motorcycle that moves 1000 m in 45 s.

4 Look carefully at this graph of a girl's journey to her village shops:

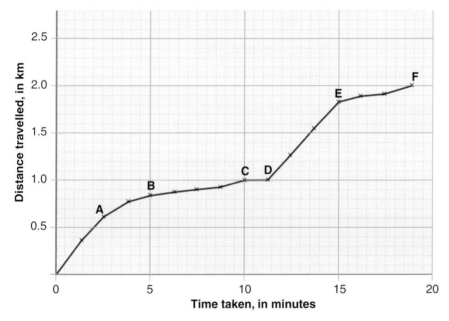

   (a) How long did the total journey take?
   (b) When did the girl stop to tie her shoelace?
   (c) Which part of the graph shows where she was walking up a steep hill?
   (d) Which part of the graph shows where she was walking downhill?
   (e) What was her average speed over the whole journey?

Extension question

5 David and Hannah were asked to observe a car moving along a marked track. They had an electronic timer and they were able to see exactly how far the car had travelled by looking at the markings on the track. They obtained these results:

Time, in seconds	0	1	2	3	4	5	6	7	8
Distance travelled, in metres	0	20	40	60	80	100	120	140	160

(a) Plot a line graph of these results.

(b) What is the car's speed in m/s?

(c) From the graph, work out how far the car would have travelled after 3.5 s.

(d) How far did the car travel between 4.0 s and 7.0 s?

(e) If the car continues at this speed, how far will it travel in 25 s?

(f) How long would it take for the car to cover 400 m?

(g) Was the car moving uphill, downhill, or along the level? Give a reason for your answer.

The force of gravity

Gravity is a **force of attraction**, in other words, a **pull** between two objects.

Everyone knows that objects fall when they are dropped. If you throw a cricket ball or a rounders ball into the air, it will fall back towards the centre of the Earth. The force that pulls the object back towards the Earth is gravity.

Sir Isaac Newton made some observations and concluded that:

- There are forces of gravity between all objects (not just between objects and the Earth).
- The size of the gravitational force depends on the **mass** of the objects pulling on each other. This means the greater the mass of the objects, the greater the attraction due to gravity.
- The size of the gravitational force depends also on the **distance** between the two objects. As the distance increases, the force of gravity gets less (but gravity *can* work over enormous distances).

> **Sir Isaac Newton**
>
> Sir Isaac Newton (1643–1727) was an English physicist and mathematician. He was one of the most influential scientists of all time. He is best known as the first person to describe the force of gravity. In 1687 he published his work *Philosophiae Naturalis Principia Mathematica* (*Mathematical Principles of Natural Philosophy*). This showed how gravity was a universal force that applied to all objects in all parts of the Universe.
>
> Newton famously formed his idea about gravity while sitting in the garden in the shade of some apple trees. He questioned why the falling apples always fell straight (perpendicularly) to the ground and this was the beginning of his most well-known discovery.

The Earth is a large object, so puts a pull force on other objects that are near it. The force of **gravity** has a direction, and this direction is **towards the centre of the Earth.**

Gravity exists between all objects. Even very small objects, like two tomatoes, are pulled towards each other. The force is very small, so it would be really difficult to measure it.

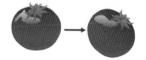

The force of gravity only becomes noticeable when one or both objects has a huge mass. The Earth's mass is about 6 000 000 000 000 000 000 000 000 kg so it has an enormous gravitational pull.

Objects pull on each other equally. A bird in the air pulls as much on the Earth as the Earth pulls on the bird. But this force will not move something as massive as the Earth!

There are two important things to remember about gravity:

- Gravity will pull an object towards the centre of the Earth, whether the object is in the air, standing on the ground or in water.
- Most places on the surface of the Earth are approximately the same distance from the centre of the Earth. Because of this, the force of gravity is almost exactly the same all over the Earth. You need to get a long way away from the Earth before you notice any real reduction in the force of gravity.

Gravity on the Moon is less than on the Earth, because the Moon is smaller. Astronauts can jump higher and longer on the Moon than on Earth.

Measuring gravity

The force of gravity acting on objects can make them feel very heavy. This heaviness as a result of gravity is the weight of an object. Because weight is a force, we can measure it using a force meter. The weight of an object should be measured in **newtons (N)**.

How to measure forces

Working Scientifically

We use a **force meter** (sometimes called a **newton meter**) (see diagram on the next page) to measure the size of a force. A force meter has a spring inside it and the larger the force, the more the spring will be stretched. The stretching of the spring changes the reading on the force meter. You can hang a weight on the hook at the bottom of a force meter. When the spring inside the force meter is stretched, it tries to pull back towards its normal length. The weight hangs in one position because this pull of the spring equals the downward pull of gravity on the weight. The two forces are **balanced.**

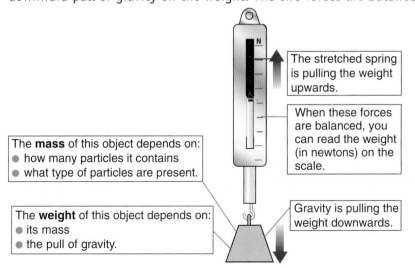

The **mass** of this object depends on:
- how many particles it contains
- what type of particles are present.

The **weight** of this object depends on:
- its mass
- the pull of gravity.

The stretched spring is pulling the weight upwards.

When these forces are balanced, you can read the weight (in newtons) on the scale.

Gravity is pulling the weight downwards.

The reading with a 1 kg mass would tell us the force of gravity in newtons.

Weight and mass

The two words weight and mass are often confused with one another. **Weight** is **the force of gravity pulling an object towards the centre of the Earth** (or some other body) and is measured in newtons (N). The **mass** of an object is **a measure of how much matter it contains** and is measured in grams or kilograms.

A kilogram mass is pulled towards the Earth by a force of 10 newtons; we say that the strength of gravity (on Earth) is 10 newtons per kilogram (10 N/kg).

If you know the mass of an object, you can calculate its weight by multiplying its mass in kilograms by the force of gravity.

weight (N) = mass (kg) × gravitational field strength (N/kg)

For example, a two-kilogram bag of flour has a weight of 2 × 10 = 20 N.

Beating the force of gravity

The Earth is very tightly packed with materials such as rocks, so gravity can't pull us through to the centre of the Earth. Gravity does tend to pull us until we reach the Earth's surface, though. We can beat gravity in three ways:

Did you know?

Gravity is different on other planets. A bag of sugar has a **mass** of 1 kg, but a **weight** of 10 N on Earth.

On the Moon the force of gravity is only one-sixth of that of Earth, so the sugar's **mass** is still 1 kg, but its **weight** is now $\frac{1}{6} \times 10 = 1.67$ N.

1 **By exerting a force in the opposite direction.** This could involve using a rocket motor that burns fuel to push it against the force of gravity.

2 **Using an upward force to support you.** This is an example of a reaction force. This could involve something as simple as standing on a chair.

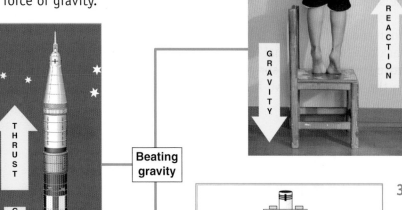

Beating gravity

3 **Using the upthrust of water.** Water pushes up against objects that are floating in it. This cancels out some of the force of gravity pulling the object to the centre of the Earth. An object will float when the force of gravity is balanced by the upthrust of water.

1 Complete these sentences using words from the following list:

grams or kg   **newtons**   **size**   **mass**   **gravity**

Weight is a force and is measured in _____ . It is caused by _____ acting on an object. _____ is not a force; it depends on the number and _____ of particles in an object. Mass is measured in _____ .

2 On Earth, the force of gravity is about 10 newtons per kg. Use this information to complete this table:

Mass, in kg	Weight, in newtons
2.0	
	15
3.7	
5.5	
	92

3 Why is there less force of gravity between two apples than between the Earth and one apple?

| Working Scientifically

Balanced and unbalanced forces

You have learned that a force is a push or a pull and that a force has both size and direction.

Keeping still: balanced forces

If an object isn't moving, then the forces on it must be balanced.

Here is a jaguar lying on a branch.

The force of gravity acts downwards on the jaguar, towards the centre of the Earth; this is the jaguar's weight. The jaguar isn't moving, so the branch must be pushing back against the jaguar with a reaction force. This force must be equal in size to the jaguar's weight, but is acting in the opposite direction.

Moving at a constant speed

An object that is *moving at a constant speed* also has balanced forces acting on it.

Balanced forces can still be acting on an object even if it is not still. A moving object with balanced forces acting on it will keep moving at exactly the same speed all the time. A car travelling along a straight road will move at a constant speed, so long as the force provided by the engine balances the air resistance and the friction from the road.

FORCE PRODUCED BY ENGINE

AIR RESISTANCE

FRICTION

Speed with no friction

We can investigate the speed of an object moving with almost no friction by using an air track. This is a metal tube that can act as a track for a trolley.

- Air is pushed up through the track to make a cushion for the trolley.
- Light gates are used to check the speed of the vehicle as it moves along the track.

> Even with no friction the trolley would eventually stop due to **air resistance** – but the track would need to be very long!

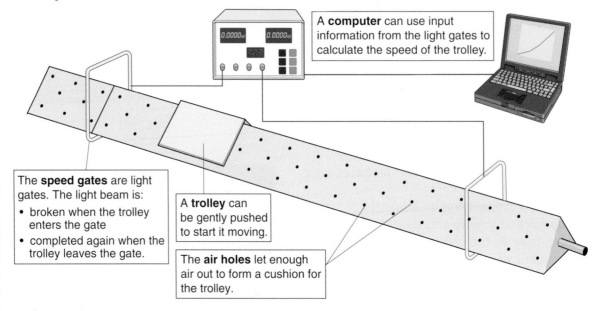

A **computer** can use input information from the light gates to calculate the speed of the trolley.

The **speed gates** are light gates. The light beam is:
- broken when the trolley enters the gate
- completed again when the trolley leaves the gate.

A **trolley** can be gently pushed to start it moving.

The **air holes** let enough air out to form a cushion for the trolley.

> **Did you know?**
> Engineers use air cushions like this to reduce the forces (friction) that slow down the movement of some machines, for example a hovercraft.

Changing speed and direction

Sometimes the forces acting on an object are **unbalanced**. Unbalanced forces can change the speed or direction of motion of an object. Let's think about what would happen to a spaceship travelling so far out into space that there is no longer any gravitational force acting on it. The spaceship has no engine to push it and no gravity or friction to slow it down. The spaceship will just travel on and on at the same speed and in the same direction.

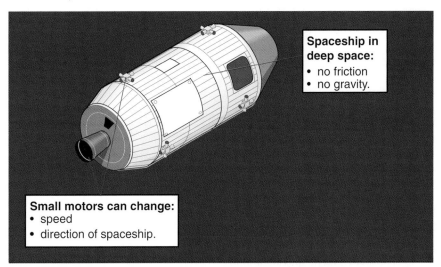

Spaceship in deep space:
• no friction
• no gravity.

Small motors can change:
• speed
• direction of spaceship.

The spaceship's speed or direction could be altered by firing little rockets fixed to it. If the rockets provide an extra force in the same direction as the spaceship is travelling, the spaceship's speed will increase. If the rockets fired in the opposite direction, the spaceship would slow down.

Acceleration tells us how fast the speed or direction of something is changing. A great acceleration requires a large, unbalanced force to be acting on an object. These rockets could also be used to manoeuvre a spaceship or satellite into the correct position for it to carry out its job. The rockets would now be providing an unbalanced force in a different *direction* from the travel of the spaceship. Unbalanced forces can change the speed or the direction of movement of an object, or even both at the same time.

■ The risk of dangerously unbalanced forces!

Many of you will probably already have carried out your own experiments on unbalanced forces. For example, when your mum or dad tries to push a supermarket trolley, you can change its direction by pushing from the side.

If the forces on an object are unbalanced this is what will happen:

• an object that is not moving starts to move
• an object that is moving changes speed or direction.

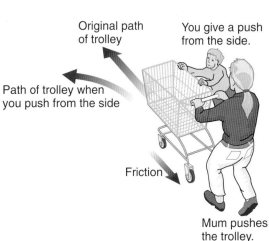

Original path of trolley

You give a push from the side.

Path of trolley when you push from the side

Friction

Mum pushes the trolley.

Resultant forces

The size of the overall force acting on an object is called the **resultant force**. If the forces are balanced, this is zero. In the example below, the resultant force is the difference between the two forces, which is:

$$100 - 60 = 40\,N$$

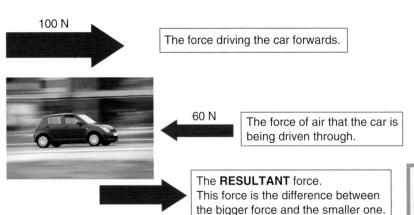

100 N

| The force driving the car forwards. |

60 N

| The force of air that the car is being driven through. |

| The **RESULTANT** force. This force is the difference between the bigger force and the smaller one. |

WHICH ONE WINS?
Remember: when two different forces work on the same object, the BIGGEST ONE WINS.

Go further

How does mass affect acceleration?

The acceleration of an object depends on the size of the force acting on it and on the **mass** of the object.

The best acceleration is obtained by either reducing the mass of the object or by increasing the force used to move it. Designers of racing cars and motorbikes understand this and they try to get the lightest vehicle and the most powerful engine.

Drag racers, for example, have:

- large powerful engines
- very light bodies
- very light alloy wheels.

All these factors combine to enable drag-racing cars to accelerate to 60 m/s in 5 seconds.

Remember: The mass of an object is a measure of how much matter it contains. It is measured in grams (g) or kilograms (kg). It is unaffected by gravity so your mass is the same whether you are on Earth or on the Moon, where there is no gravity.

Don't confuse mass with **weight**. Weight is force of gravity pulling on an object towards the centre of the Earth (or some other large body). It is measured in newtons (N). You would weigh less on the Moon than you do on Earth.

Investigation: Stretching materials

The aim of this experiment is to investigate how the extension (stretching) of a material is affected by the degree of force that is applied.

Safety: You must wear safety goggles when carrying out this experiment.

The diagram below shows how to set up your experiment. You can choose to investigate the stretching of a rubber band or a spring.

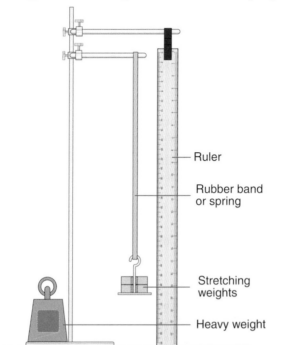

Ruler

Rubber band or spring

Stretching weights

Heavy weight

1. Think about the experiment you are about to carry out and write down the independent (input) variable, the dependent (outcome) variable.
2. Write down any other things that could affect the outcome. These are the control variables.

Start the experiment.

● Start off with no weights on your spring/rubber band. Look at eye level and find the position of the spring/rubber band against the ruler when there are no weights attached. Try to find the position to the nearest millimetre. Using a small ruler to check that you are looking on the level would help. Record the length of the spring/rubber band in the 0 N row in a suitable table using the headings provided below.

Weight, in newtons	Position of bottom spring or rubber band, in cm	Extension, in cm
0		

- Decide on the heaviest weight that you will use. Your heaviest weight should be safe to use and should produce an extension of at least 20 cm.
- Now decide whether you should increase the weight by 0.5 N between readings or by 1 N between readings.
- Now increase the weight by one step (0.5 N or 1 N, whatever you decided).
- Find the new position of the end of the spring/rubber band and record this length in the table.
- Calculate the extension and record this in the table.
- Go through the last three steps again until you have used your heaviest weight.

3 Plot your results on a graph showing weight against extension.
4 What happens to the spring/rubber band when the force that you apply to it is increased?

If you have time, carry out the experiment with the spring/rubber band, the one you did not use first time around. Alternatively, half the class could investigate the spring and the other half could investigate the rubber band.

5 After discussion with your teacher, sketch results on graphs to show the general pattern found by the class for (a) the spring and (b) the rubber band.
6 (a) What must happen to the particles in the spring or in the rubber band when it extends?
  (b) What happens to the particles when you remove the force from the object?
7 (a) What might happen to the spring if you applied a very strong force to it?
  (b) What must happen to the particles when the spring is overstretched?
8 (a) What happens to the rubber band when you apply a strong force to it, but not enough to make it snap?
  (b) Can you explain this in terms of the particles that are inside it?

Stretching the limits

The spring in a force meter will stretch, depending on the mass added.

   Hooke's law states that: **The amount of stretch is proportional to the mass added.**

   Usually the spring will stretch the same amount if identical masses are added, and will go back to its original position if the mass is taken off it. We say that the spring is **elastic** (the material we call elastic is called this because it returns to its original length after it has been stretched). Something unusual can happen if you keep on and on adding mass. The spring will suddenly stretch much more than expected and it won't go back to its original length once the mass is removed. Scientists say that we have exceeded the **elastic limits** of the material. Hooke's law is *not* obeyed in this situation. This is shown on the next page:

On this side of the graph:
- the extension of the spring is **proportional** to the added weight
- removing the weight will see the spring returning to its original position.

At 5 N the spring goes beyond its **elastic limit** and the graph is beyond the **limit of proportionality.**

- The extension of the spring is now **not** proportional to the added weight.
- The spring will not return to its original position.

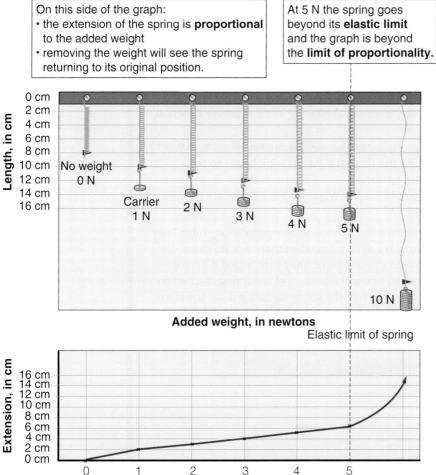

Added weight, in newtons

Elastic limit of spring

Added weight, in newtons

■ A spring has an elastic limit.

When they are using materials, engineers must be very careful that they don't exceed the elastic limits for the materials they are using. It might have disastrous consequences.

Changing shape

Elastic objects can also store elastic potential energy when they are squashed. For example, this happens when a tennis ball is dropped onto a hard surface.

The potential energy will allow the ball to return to its original shape.

1 Make a drawing of a car accelerating away from traffic lights. Draw the force arrows to show the forces acting on the car.

2 Sir Bradley Wiggins is a racing cyclist who became the first British cyclist to win the Tour de France. On one stage of this race he was pedalling with a force equivalent to 120 N but the wind was blowing in the opposite direction with a force of 15 N.

Working Scientifically

(a) What is the value of the resultant force moving Bradley Wiggins forward?

(b) As the cyclists turned into the final straight the wind began to blow harder. Its force increased to 40 N.
How much extra force would Bradley Wiggins have to generate in order to keep up the same speed?

3 Two students hung a spring from a strong support alongside a long ruler. They measured where the bottom of the spring was when there was no metal disc added to the spring; this was the starting point. They then added different discs to the spring and measured where the bottom of the spring reached on the scale. They worked out the stretch of the spring by taking away the starting point from the finishing point each time.
Here are their results:

Mass of added discs, in grams	Position of spring, in millimetres	Amount of stretch, in millimetres (extension)
0	12	0
10	22	
20	35	
30	48	
40	60	
50	73	
60	85	
70	97	85
80	110	
90	122	
100	136	
110	149	
120	160	

(a) Complete the table by working out the amount of stretch (extension) for each added disc.

(b) Plot a graph of the added mass against the stretch of the spring.

(c) What is the pattern in these results?

(d) Use your graph to find out how much the spring would have stretched with a load of 58 g. Show your working on the graph.

(e) What load would be needed to stretch the spring by 102 cm? Show your working on the graph.

(f) What do you think would happen if the two students kept adding discs to the spring? Draw a simple graph that they might get. Explain this result.

Extension questions

4 A shuttle can be used to put satellites and measuring equipment into orbit. An empty shuttle vehicle has a mass of 70 tonnes and can carry a cargo of 28 tonnes. (1 tonne = 1000 kilograms)

   (a) What is the total mass of the full shuttle, in kilograms?
   (b) What is the weight of the shuttle as it sits on the launch pad?
   (c) How much force (thrust) would the rockets have to produce just to balance this weight at take-off?

5 This equation can be used to calculate the rate of change of speed (acceleration) in m per s per s (m/s^2).

$$\text{Acceleration} = \frac{\text{change in speed}}{\text{time taken}}$$

This table shows how the speed of a motorcycle changes over a 5-second period.

Time, in seconds	0	1	2	3	4	5
Speed, in metres per second	0	4	8	12	16	20

   (a) What is the acceleration of the motorbike?
   (b) If the motorbike keeps on accelerating at this rate, how fast will it be going after:
        (i)   9 seconds?
        (ii) 20 seconds?
   (c) Why would it be difficult to predict how fast the motorbike would be going after 50 seconds?

Friction and motion

As you have learned, moving objects often slow down because there is a force acting on them. The force is acting in the opposite direction to the way the objects are moving. This force is called friction.

Friction: pros and cons

Friction is a force that tends to stop two things from sliding over each other. Sometimes friction is useful:

- Car tyres can push against the surface of the road, so the car can move forward.
- Brake blocks can squeeze against a bicycle wheel rim, so that the bike slows down.
- Shoes can grip the floor, so that you don't slip when you try to walk.

However, sometimes friction is a nuisance:

- It slows moving things down, and extra force is needed to keep them moving.
- It can heat things up and can damage the moving surfaces.

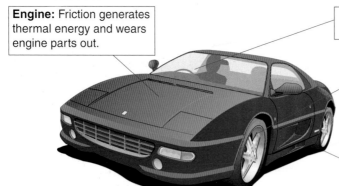

Friction can be a nuisance!

Engine: Friction generates thermal energy and wears engine parts out.

Friction can be useful!

Steering wheel and driving gloves: These make it easier to hold on and steer the car.

Brake pads and discs: Friction between them will slow the car down.

Tyres and ground: Friction means:
- the engine can push car forward
- grip means the car will stick to the ground and will stop the car when braking
- the car can be made to change direction.

Brakes, tyres, roads and friction

Driving a car or motorbike safely would be impossible without friction. Especially important is the friction between the tyres and the road. When the driver or rider puts on the brakes, the wheels stop turning and the vehicle will slow down as long as the tyres can grip the road. The grip between the tyre and the road depends on friction. This friction can be affected by:

- The type of road surface. Some surfaces are specially roughened to provide good friction and safe braking.
- Whether the road is wet or not. Water acts as a lubricant (see How to reduce friction, later in this chapter) between the tyre and the road and makes braking more difficult.
- The condition of the tyres. Worn tyres are smooth and so friction with the road is reduced, especially in wet conditions.

This diagram shows how braking is affected by the condition of the road. Assume a driver of a car travelling at 80 km per hour (50 mph) wants to stop his car.

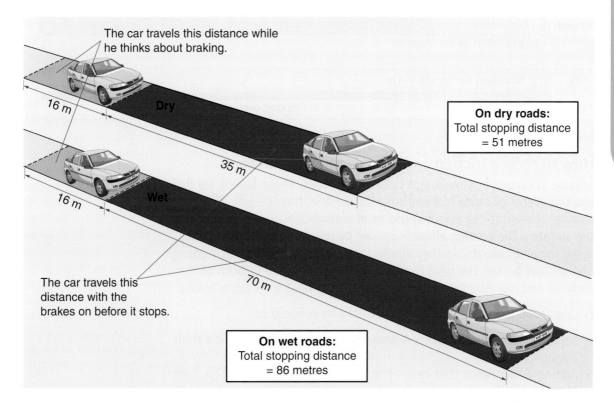

The car travels this distance while he thinks about braking.

16 m

Dry

On dry roads:
Total stopping distance
= 51 metres

35 m

16 m

Wet

The car travels this distance with the brakes on before it stops.

70 m

On wet roads:
Total stopping distance
= 86 metres

Speed and braking

Even when a car has perfect tyres and brakes and the road is dry, stopping a car can be very difficult. The faster a car is travelling, the longer it will take for it to stop. This is because the car will travel further while the driver reacts to the situation, and also because the friction must act for longer to stop the car moving forward.

The UK Highway Code shows the distances required for braking at different speeds. At 60 mph (96.6 km per hour) under perfect conditions, stopping the car still takes nearly 20 times the length of the car.

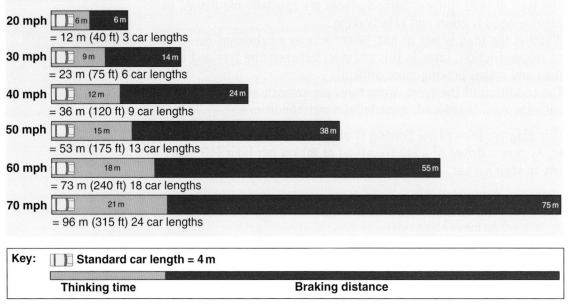

20 mph | 6 m | 6 m
= 12 m (40 ft) 3 car lengths

30 mph | 9 m | 14 m
= 23 m (75 ft) 6 car lengths

40 mph | 12 m | 24 m
= 36 m (120 ft) 9 car lengths

50 mph | 15 m | 38 m
= 53 m (175 ft) 13 car lengths

60 mph | 18 m | 55 m
= 73 m (240 ft) 18 car lengths

70 mph | 21 m | 75 m
= 96 m (315 ft) 24 car lengths

Key: **Standard car length = 4 m**

Thinking time | **Braking distance**

■ Speed affects braking distance

How to reduce friction and stop damage to surfaces

Friction is caused by tiny bumps between surfaces. These bumps are just like tiny pieces of sandpaper and stop the surfaces from moving. They also damage the surface by scraping pieces of material away and by heating the surfaces. The heating effect is caused by the particles in the surface being forced to vibrate. As they vibrate, they will have more kinetic energy and will get hotter. The heat can be enough to melt one or both of the surfaces and can stop the materials from carrying out their job properly.

Friction, and the damage it can cause, can be reduced by:

● Smoothing off the surfaces. A smooth surface has less friction than a rough one.
● Adding a substance that keeps the surfaces slightly apart. This kind of substance is called a lubricant. Good examples are grease or oil.

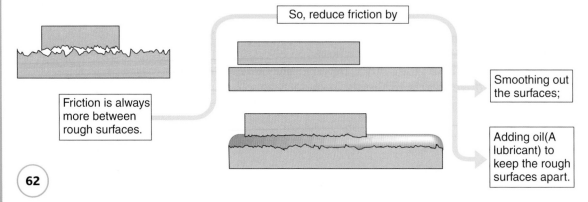

So, reduce friction by

Friction is always more between rough surfaces.

Smoothing out the surfaces;

Adding oil(A lubricant) to keep the rough surfaces apart.

Air resistance is a kind of friction

Air resistance (also called drag) is a kind of friction between a moving object and the air. Drag acts on you as you cycle along the road. The amount of drag can be reduced by making the object more streamlined. A streamlined object is shaped so that the air can flow smoothly past it. This reduces the air resistance so that the object can move more quickly through the air.

Air resistance and thermal energy

When an object moves through the air, it will make the particles of the air move about. This can be very serious. The space shuttle, for example, generated an enormous amount of thermal energy when it re-entered the Earth's atmosphere. Some of this thermal energy was transferred back to the spacecraft, making it glow 'white hot'. The shuttle would have been severely damaged by this massive amount of thermal energy if it did not have protection from the special tiles that covered it. This heating effect, together with damage to the tile covering (which happened on take-off), caused the disastrous break-up of the space shuttle *Columbia* in 2003, resulting in the deaths of all seven crew members.

■ This motorbike would meet a lot of air resistance

■ This motorbike is streamlined to reduce wind resistance. The same amount of force will make this one go faster than the one above.

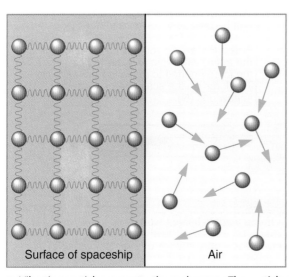

Surface of spaceship   Air

■ Vibrating particles generate thermal energy. The particles on the surface of the shuttle are fixed in place, so no thermal energy is generated by vibration.

■ The space shuttle (NASA 1981–2011) was covered in thermal-resistant tiles made of silica. These protected it from the thermal energy generated by friction as it re-entered the atmosphere from space. The tiles became heated until they were white hot (see at the nose at upper right).

Movement through water

As well as air, water also provides resistance to the motion of objects and living things through it.

The streamlined shapes that help to reduce air resistance also help in movement through water.

The evolution (see Biology, Chapter 9) of living organisms that live in water has provided many excellent examples of streamlining. Some of these are so effective that humans have copied them.

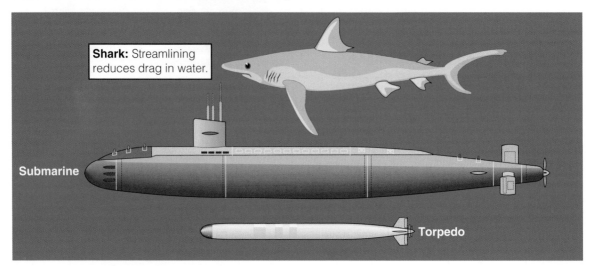

Shark: Streamlining reduces drag in water.

Submarine

Torpedo

Because friction is a force, it too can be measured using a force meter. The way that this is done is shown in the diagram. Measurements of friction between different kinds of surface must be done as a fair test.

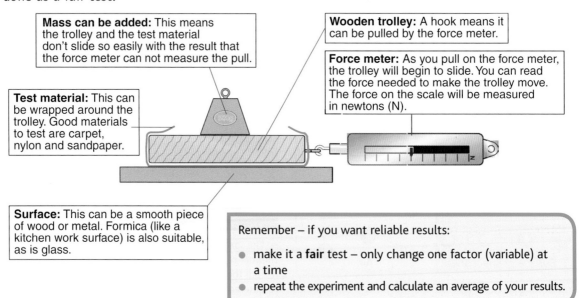

Mass can be added: This means the trolley and the test material don't slide so easily with the result that the force meter can not measure the pull.

Wooden trolley: A hook means it can be pulled by the force meter.

Force meter: As you pull on the force meter, the trolley will begin to slide. You can read the force needed to make the trolley move. The force on the scale will be measured in newtons (N).

Test material: This can be wrapped around the trolley. Good materials to test are carpet, nylon and sandpaper.

Surface: This can be a smooth piece of wood or metal. Formica (like a kitchen work surface) is also suitable, as is glass.

Remember – if you want reliable results:

- make it a **fair** test – only change one factor (variable) at a time
- repeat the experiment and calculate an average of your results.

Investigation: Measuring friction

The aim of this experiment is to investigate friction.

Your group will be provided with a friction sledge or block of wood (as shown on the previous page), some weights, a force meter and a set of surfaces (materials) that you can attach to the bottom of the sledge. The surfaces are polythene, J cloth, sandpaper, carpet, denim cloth (or any other materials that your teacher has provided you with).

Your task is to investigate how the surface on the bottom of the sledge affects the force that is needed to pull the sledge across the lab bench.

1 Write down the independent (input) variable, the dependent (outcome) variable.
2 Write down any other things that could affect the outcome. These are the control variables.

Before you begin to take readings from the apparatus you must do some preliminary work to find out what values of controlled variables to use. See how to attach the surfaces to the sledge and find out which surface is the most slippery and which is the least slippery.

Now find out what is a suitable weight to put on your sledge. You want the slipperiest surface to need enough force for you to be able to measure it. Check that you are using the best force meter for the job. You will need to be able to measure the force that is needed to pull the sledge across the bench at a steady speed. Practice pulling the sledge steadily. Create a suitable table using the headings below, and record the value of the force used.

Surface	Force needed to pull sledge steadily in newtons		
	Reading 1	Reading 2	Average

Now test the least slippery surface under the same conditions. You may need to use a different force meter. Record the force.

Test each of the other surfaces in turn. Make sure that you are always using the force meter that is most appropriate for the task and record the value of the force in the table.

Repeat your tests on each surface making sure you record your results. Then work out the average value of the force needed.

3 Represent your results in a bar chart.
4 (a) Which was the most difficult surface for the sledge to move on?
   (b) Represent the surfaces in a drawing to explain your findings.

Exercise 4.1: Friction

1 State the names of two friction forces that would slow down a bicycle.

2 State two things that always happen when friction takes place.

3 Which of the following statements does **not** describe air resistance?
   (a) It is also called drag.   (c) It helps streamlined cars to move quickly.
   (b) It is a kind of friction.   (d) It produces thermal energy.

4 This diagram shows two of the forces acting on a remote-controlled model car when it is moving.

Friction

Forward force

(a) When the motor was switched off, the car slowed down and then stopped. While the car was slowing down, which of the statements **(i)** to **(iii)** was true?

(i) Forward force and friction were both greater than zero.

(ii) Friction was zero and the forward force was zero.

(iii) The forward force was zero and the friction was greater than zero.

(b) Look at the distance–time graph. What was the time when the car started to slow down?

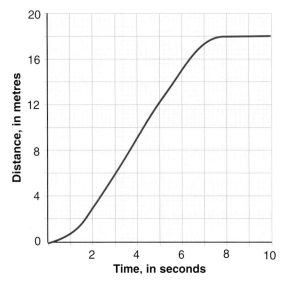

5 A scientist wants to try different test materials to see how much friction there is with the wheels of a toy car. She set up her 'U'-shaped track.

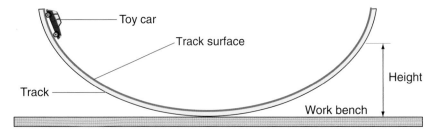

Toy car

Track surface

Height

Track

Work bench

(a) Which of the following, **(i)** to **(iv)**, would achieve a fair test? Give reasons for your answer.

   (i) Using two cars, one with steel wheels and one with rubber wheels. The test material is a piece of cotton.

   (ii) Using a car with rubber wheels and three different test materials: writing paper, carpet and sandpaper.

   (iii) Using two cars and two different types of sandpaper as the test material, one smooth and one very rough.

   (iv) Using two different pieces of woollen cloth, one car and two different 'U'-shaped tracks.

(b) The scientist decides to use a car with rubber wheels, one 'U'-shaped track and four different materials: carpet, writing paper, a woollen blanket and some rough sandpaper. For each test she released the car from the same place on the track and measured the height it reached on the opposite side of the 'U'-shaped track from the work bench. The results are shown below:

Type of material	Mean height reached, in cm (after 10 tries)
Carpet	12
Writing paper	40
Woollen blanket	26
Rough sandpaper	32

   (i) Which surface provided the least friction?

   (ii) Which surface provided the most friction?

   (iii) Why did the scientist repeat the experiment ten times for each material?

Extension question

6 A motorcyclist is travelling at 25 m/s (nearly 60 mph) on a dual carriageway when he notices that there has been an accident 70 metres in front of him. He takes 0.5 s to react before squeezing the brakes. The brakes take 3 s to stop the motorbike.

(a) Draw a speed–time graph from the time he notices the accident to the time the motorbike stops.

(b) What was his total stopping distance?

(c) What do you think happened?

Hint: to find the stopping distance you will need to calculate the **area** under the speed–time graph.

5 More on forces

You have learned that a force can cause an object to change its **speed** or **direction** of movement. This change could include making a stationary object move or a moving object come to rest.

Forces and rotation

Forces can also have a turning effect; for example, a spanner can be used to turn a bolt, or a lever can be used to lift a load. These tools create a turning effect around a pivot. Spanners and levers can be used to increase turning effects.

A lever is any rigid body that is able to turn about a pivot.

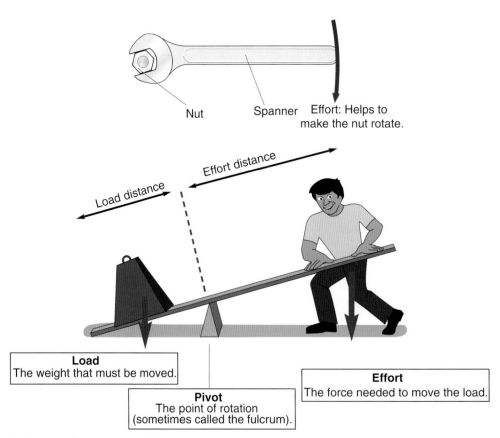

Nut   Spanner   Effort: Helps to make the nut rotate.

Effort distance

Load distance

Load
The weight that must be moved.

Pivot
The point of rotation (sometimes called the fulcrum).

Effort
The force needed to move the load.

■ Forces can have a turning effect

The size of the turning effect

As well as changing the direction of a force, a lever can change the **magnitude** of a force. The size or strength of a turning effect is called a moment. The moment depends on the **amount of effort used** and on the **distance between the effort and the pivot**. It is calculated using the formula:

Turning effect (moment) = effort (force) × distance to pivot

Can't budge it!

Remember the units:

- force (N)
- distance (m)

Easy peasy

Therefore the units for moments (turning forces) are called newton-metres (N m) (or newton centimetres, N cm).

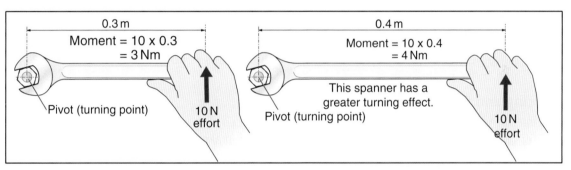

0.3 m
Moment = 10 x 0.3
= 3 N m

Pivot (turning point)

10 N effort

0.4 m
Moment = 10 x 0.4
= 4 N m

This spanner has a greater turning effect.

Pivot (turning point)

10 N effort

A **longer** lever gives a **bigger** turning force.

Everyday levers

Humans use this lever effect in many ways. Some everyday levers are shown here:

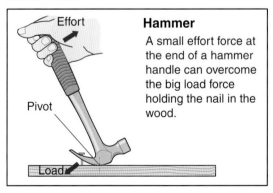

Effort

Pivot

Load

Hammer

A small effort force at the end of a hammer handle can overcome the big load force holding the nail in the wood.

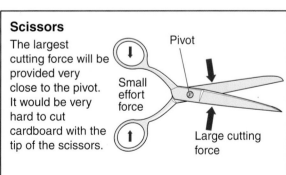

Scissors

The largest cutting force will be provided very close to the pivot. It would be very hard to cut cardboard with the tip of the scissors.

Pivot

Small effort force

Large cutting force

Here are some more everyday levers:

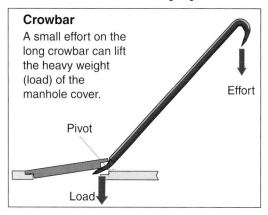

Crowbar
A small effort on the long crowbar can lift the heavy weight (load) of the manhole cover.

Effort

Pivot

Load

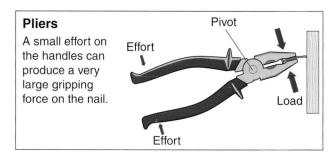

Pliers
A small effort on the handles can produce a very large gripping force on the nail.

Effort

Pivot

Load

Effort

We sometimes refer to these levers as 'simple machines'. These simple machines all give a force greater than the force applied, but at the expense of smaller movement. For example, the 'effort' end of the crowbar in the diagram above must move over a greater distance than the 'load' end. In the same way, an enormous effort would be required if the distance between effort and pivot was very short – this is not very common in simple machines.

Balancing and moments

Sometimes it is important that turning forces are balanced. For example, two people sitting on a see-saw might want to make it possible for both of them to move equally easily. This will only be possible if the moment in one direction is balanced by the moment in the other direction, as explained below:

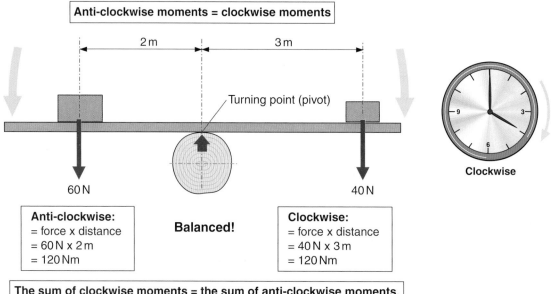

Anti-clockwise moments = clockwise moments

2 m   3 m

Turning point (pivot)

60 N   40 N

Clockwise

Anti-clockwise:
= force x distance
= 60 N x 2 m
= 120 Nm

Balanced!

Clockwise:
= force x distance
= 40 N x 3 m
= 120 Nm

The sum of clockwise moments = the sum of anti-clockwise moments.

You can see from this example that one weight has a turning effect to the left and one has a turning effect to the right. If the two turning effects are equal, the ruler will be balanced. This is an example of the Law of Moments:

Moment turning to the left = moment turning to the right

Investigation: Strength of moments

Working Scientifically

The aim of this experiment is to investigate the strength of a turning effect called a moment.

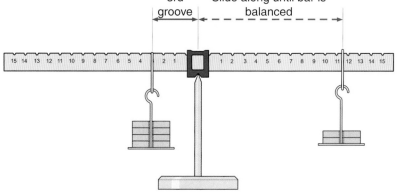

3rd groove Slide along until bar is balanced

The moments apparatus is like the balancing bar shown in the diagram above, but you can also balance an ordinary metre ruler.

- Assemble your apparatus without any weights. Ensure that the bar balances in a horizontal position.
- To start with, you are going to test the arrangement of weights indicated in the top row of the table below. Put four weights into hole 3 on the left-hand side of the bar. Now take two weights and, by trial and error, find where they must be put on the right-hand side so that the bar balances. Record the hole number in row 1 of the table on the next page.

Left-hand side			Right-hand side		
Position	No. of weights		Position	No. of weights	
3	4		2		
2	3		1		
5	3		3		
8	3		4		

1 Notice that there is a blank column for both the right- and left-hand sides of the bar. Your challenge is to decide what goes into these columns during the course of the experiment.

Now test the arrangement shown in row 2 of the table: three weights in hole 2 on the left-hand side balanced with one weight on the right.

Work through the rest of the examples. When you see a pattern, make up some examples of your own and test them. The bottom two rows are for your own tests.

2 State the law of moments.

3 State the correct units to describe moments.

Go further

Centre of gravity and stability

A ruler will balance without any additional weights if it is supported at its midpoint. This is because the weights of all the particles on one side of the pivot are balanced by the weights of all the particles on the other side of the pivot. It seems as if all of the weight of the ruler is acting through just one point. This point is called the centre of gravity (or the centre of mass).

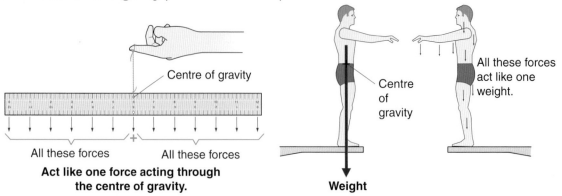

Centre of gravity

All these forces
Act like one force acting through the centre of gravity.

Centre of gravity

All these forces act like one weight.

Weight

Some objects fall over very easily when they are pushed. This is because they are unstable. A stable object is much more difficult to topple. How stable an object is depends on how far we can tip it before its centre of gravity is moved outside its base.

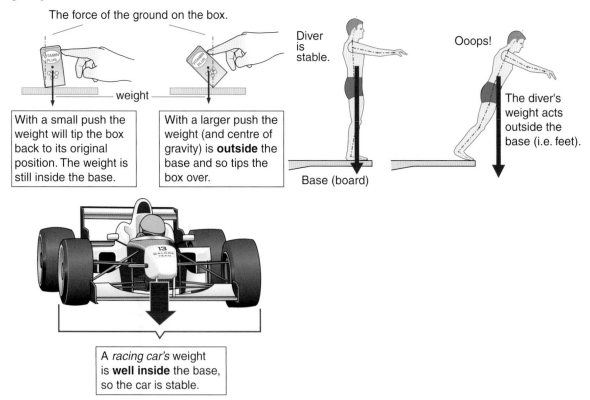

The force of the ground on the box.

weight

With a small push the weight will tip the box back to its original position. The weight is still inside the base.

With a larger push the weight (and centre of gravity) is **outside** the base and so tips the box over.

Diver is stable.

Base (board)

Ooops!

The diver's weight acts outside the base (i.e. feet).

A *racing car's* weight is **well inside** the base, so the car is stable.

5 *More on forces*

Exercise 5.1: Forces and rotation

1 Look at these diagrams:

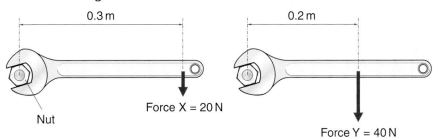

Force X = 20 N

Nut

Force Y = 40 N

(a) Which of the forces, X or Y, has the greater turning effect? Explain your answer.
(b) How could you increase the turning effect of Y?

2 Make a drawing to explain the meaning of each of these words.

Working Scientifically

(a) Pivot   (d) Effort
(b) Load   (e) Load distance
(c) Moment   (f) Effort distance

3 Write down the formula for calculating a moment. Show how the formula can be extended to describe the Law of Moments.

Extension question

4 The diagram below shows a crane. The crane has a movable counter-balance that can be moved to any position up to 2 m from the pivot.

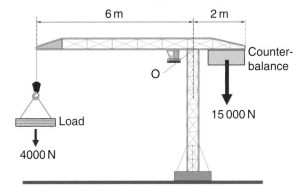

6 m

2 m

Counter-balance

O

Load

15 000 N

4000 N

(a) Why does the crane need a counterbalance?
(b) Why must the counterbalance be movable?
(c) What is the moment of the 4000 N force (about point O)?
(d) If the crane is balanced when the 4000 N load is being lifted, what moment must the 15 000 N force have?
(e) How far from O should the counterbalance be placed?
(f) What is the maximum load (in N) the crane should lift?

Force and pressure

You may have heard the word **pressure** in connection with the force exerted by gas particles on the walls of a container (see Chemistry, Chapter 1). Pressure can also be used to describe the force exerted by a solid or by a liquid.

Pressure is a way of describing how concentrated a force is. Pressure therefore depends on two things:

- how **big** the force is
- how **large an area** the force is working on.

Here we will look at pressure of solids. We will look at liquids in the next section.

The diagram below shows a drawing pin being pushed into a noticeboard. Although the pushing force generated by the muscles in the thumb does not change, there are other pressures that exist:

- The pressure on the head of the drawing pin and on the tip of the thumb. This pressure is **low** because the force is spread out over a **large area**.
- The pressure on the tip of the pin and on the noticeboard. This pressure is **high**. This is because the force has been concentrated over a **small area**.

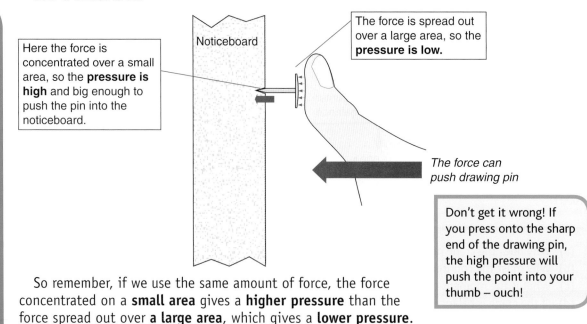

Here the force is concentrated over a small area, so the **pressure is high** and big enough to push the pin into the noticeboard.

Noticeboard

The force is spread out over a large area, so the **pressure is low.**

The force can push drawing pin

Don't get it wrong! If you press onto the sharp end of the drawing pin, the high pressure will push the point into your thumb – ouch!

So remember, if we use the same amount of force, the force concentrated on a **small area** gives a **higher pressure** than the force spread out over **a large area**, which gives a **lower pressure**.

Pressure in everyday situations

There are many occasions when an understanding of force, area and pressure can be useful. Some of these are shown below:

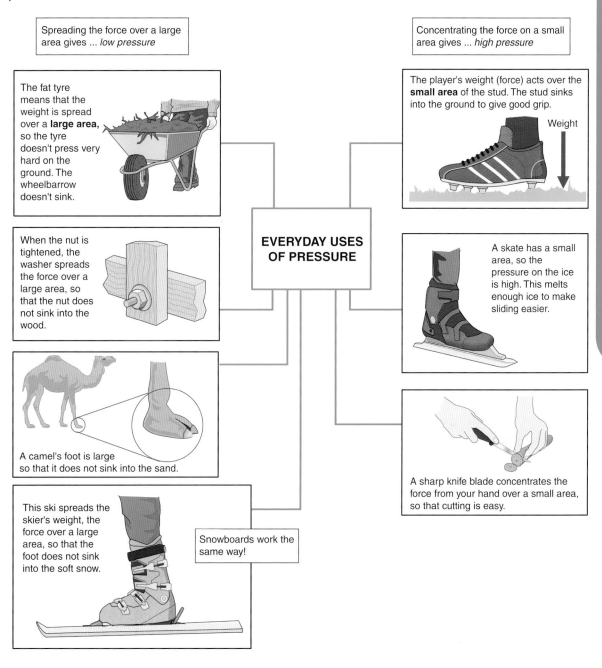

Spreading the force over a large area gives ... *low pressure*

Concentrating the force on a small area gives ... *high pressure*

The fat tyre means that the weight is spread over a **large area,** so the tyre doesn't press very hard on the ground. The wheelbarrow doesn't sink.

The player's weight (force) acts over the **small area** of the stud. The stud sinks into the ground to give good grip.

Weight

When the nut is tightened, the washer spreads the force over a large area, so that the nut does not sink into the wood.

EVERYDAY USES OF PRESSURE

A skate has a small area, so the pressure on the ice is high. This melts enough ice to make sliding easier.

A camel's foot is large so that it does not sink into the sand.

A sharp knife blade concentrates the force from your hand over a small area, so that cutting is easy.

This ski spreads the skier's weight, the force over a large area, so that the foot does not sink into the soft snow.

Snowboards work the same way!

Calculating pressure

The pressure caused by a force is calculated using the formula:

$$\textbf{Pressure} = \frac{\textbf{force}}{\textbf{area}}$$

As you know, force is measured in newtons (N) and area is measured in square metres (m²) or square centimetres (cm²); so the units for pressure will be newtons per square metre (N/m²) or newtons per square centimetre (N/cm²).

Here are some examples of calculating pressure:

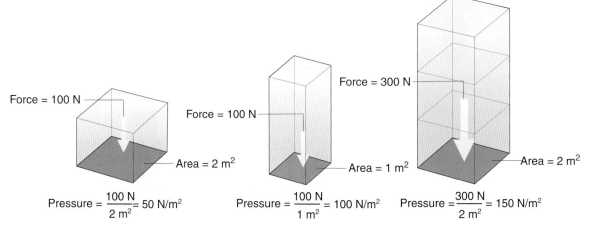

Force = 100 N — Area = 2 m²

$$\text{Pressure} = \frac{100\ \text{N}}{2\ \text{m}^2} = 50\ \text{N/m}^2$$

This block exerts a pressure of 50 N/m².

Force = 100 N — Area = 1 m²

$$\text{Pressure} = \frac{100\ \text{N}}{1\ \text{m}^2} = 100\ \text{N/m}^2$$

The pressure is now 100 N/m² because the same force is pressing on a smaller area (half the size).

Force = 300 N — Area = 2 m²

$$\text{Pressure} = \frac{300\ \text{N}}{2\ \text{m}^2} = 150\ \text{N/m}^2$$

The pressure here is 150 N/m². The force is three times bigger than the first example.

Calculating force or area

Sometimes you might need to calculate the force or the area when you are given a value for the pressure. You can rearrange the pressure formula above to give these two formulae:

Force = pressure × area   and   **Area = force/pressure**

You might find it easier to use a pressure triangle in calculations like this. One of these is shown here:

To use it, cover up the letter you need to calculate and you will see the formula. So if you need to calculate the force causing a pressure, cover up the F like this, and you can see:

Units are sometimes given as N/cm² and sometimes as N/m². Watch out for this and make sure you give your answers with the correct units.

P × A

so

Force = pressure × area

Exercise 5.2: Pressure

1 (a) What are the units for pressure?
  (b) Write down a simple formula that will let you calculate a pressure.

2 A woman is wearing high heels. If she stands on one heel, she puts a pressure of 1200 N/cm² on the ground and each heel has a surface area of 0.5 cm². What is her weight in newtons?

Working Scientifically

3 The block in this diagram weighs 18 000 N.

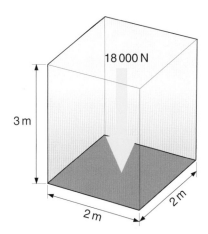

18 000 N

3 m

2 m

2 m

(a) What is the area under the block?
(b) What is the pressure under the block?
(c) If the block is tipped onto its side, what will the new pressure be?

4 Use your ideas about pressure to explain why:
  (a) It is easier to walk on soft snow if you have snowshoes rather than ice skates.
  (b) It is easier to pick up food with the prongs of a fork than with the handle.

Extension question

5 (a) What pressure do you put onto the surface of the Earth? You can calculate this by firstly working out the area of your feet by standing on some squared graph paper. You then draw around the outline of your feet and count the number of centimetre squares you cover. Then work out your weight in newtons by measuring your mass (in kg) and multiplying by 10. You should now be able to calculate the pressure you exert in N/cm².
  (b) There are 10 000 cm² in 1 m². Calculate the pressure you exert in N/m².

Go further

Pressure in liquids

You have learned that pressure is a force pushing on a certain area. Pressure is high when the force presses onto a small area and low when the force presses onto a large area. Liquids also exert pressure.

If you pour a liquid into a container, such as a bottle or jug, the weight of the liquid pushes down on the container's base. The pressure on the base can be calculated from knowing the force (weight) and the area it is acting on:

$$\text{Pressure} = \frac{\text{force}}{\text{area}}$$

There are three important points to remember about pressure in liquids:

- Pressure in a liquid increases with depth.
- Pressure at any point in a liquid acts equally in all directions.
- The shape of the container does not affect the pressure in a liquid.

These concepts are explained in the diagrams below:

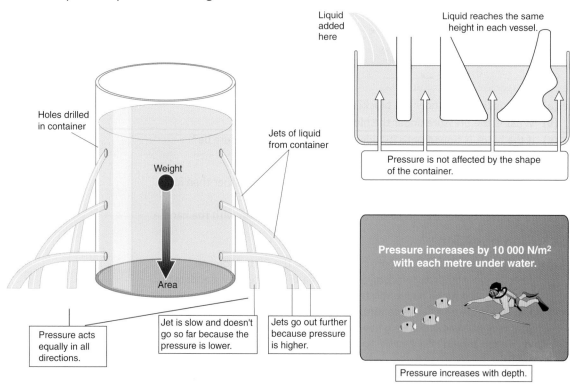

Holes drilled in container

Weight

Area

Liquid added here

Liquid reaches the same height in each vessel.

Jets of liquid from container

Pressure is not affected by the shape of the container.

Pressure acts equally in all directions.

Jet is slow and doesn't go so far because the pressure is lower.

Jets go out further because pressure is higher.

Pressure increases by 10 000 N/m² with each metre under water.

Pressure increases with depth.

Hydraulics

Liquids are very difficult to compress (squeeze). This is because their particles are very close together and there is no space between them for them to move around. This means that if you apply a force to the surface of a liquid in a container, the force will be transmitted through the liquid. This is known as hydraulic pressure, and is explained in the diagram on the next page:

5 More on forces

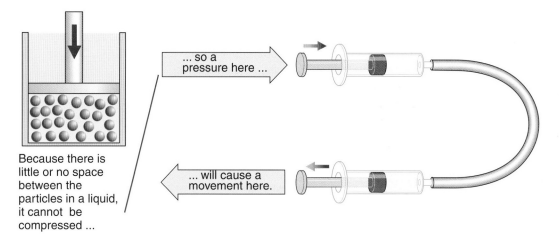

Because there is little or no space between the particles in a liquid, it cannot be compressed ...

■ Pressure is transmitted through a liquid

Humans use some of these rules about pressure in liquids to build machines that use hydraulic pressure. The hydraulic pressure is used to move pistons inside cylinders. The engineers who design the machines can use pistons of different sizes to change forces in hydraulic systems, as explained below.

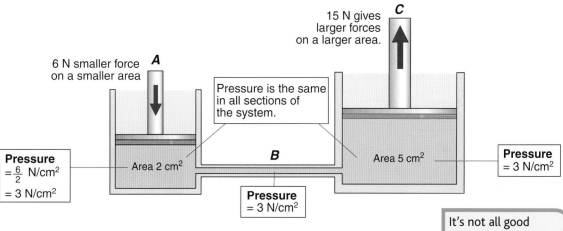

If you know the pressure and area at *C*, you can calculate the force at *C* by using the equation for pressure, which you have just learned:

It's not all good news. The larger piston will move a shorter distance.

At *C* we know that:

$$P = 3\,N/cm^2 \quad \text{and} \quad A = 5\,cm^2$$

If

$$P = \frac{F}{A}$$

Then

$$F = P \times A$$
$$= 3\,N/cm^2 \times 5\,cm^2$$
$$= 15\,N$$

So we can say that a force of 6 N at *A* causes a force of 15 N at *C*.

Hydraulics and braking

Hydraulic forces are used to operate the braking systems of cars and motorbikes. A small piston is pressed with a small force at one end of a tube, either by the brake pedal of a car or the brake lever of a motorbike. The tube, which has thick, strong walls that won't bulge under pressure, is filled with a special hydraulic fluid. The pressure in the fluid is transmitted to a larger piston, which forces brake pads onto the disc. The wheel is slowed down by the friction of the brake pads on the disc (see Chapter 4).

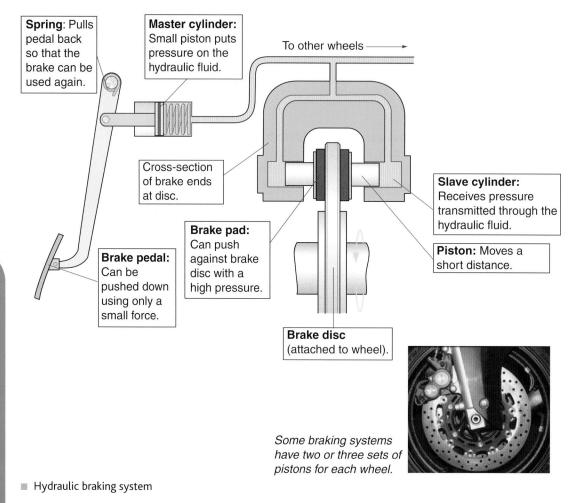

Spring: Pulls pedal back so that the brake can be used again.

Master cylinder: Small piston puts pressure on the hydraulic fluid.

To other wheels ⟶

Cross-section of brake ends at disc.

Brake pedal: Can be pushed down using only a small force.

Brake pad: Can push against brake disc with a high pressure.

Slave cylinder: Receives pressure transmitted through the hydraulic fluid.

Piston: Moves a short distance.

Brake disc (attached to wheel).

Some braking systems have two or three sets of pistons for each wheel.

■ Hydraulic braking system

6 Density

Investigation: Density

This experiment will help you to understand what is meant by density.

Density tells us how much mass is packed into each unit of volume of a material. When you are told the density, you are being told how much mass there is in either $1\,cm^3$ or $1\,m^3$.

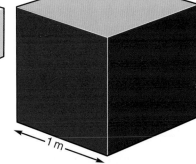

1 If you have a sample of a material with a high density then will it be heavy or light for its volume?

2 Your teacher will give you some samples of materials that have a volume of $1\,cm^3$. Find the mass of three of these and complete the table below:

Material	Mass of $1\,cm^3$	If I had:	Then the mass would be:
		$100\,cm^3$	
		$3\,cm^3$	
		$20\,cm^3$	

Solids are usually denser than liquids and liquids are denser than gases.

A kilogram of feathers has exactly the same mass as a kilogram of iron – of course. However, the kilogram of feathers will take up more space than the kilogram of iron. We say that the feathers have a lower density than the iron.

Calculating density

We can work out the density of any substance using the following equation:

$$\text{Density} = \frac{\text{mass}}{\text{volume}}$$

where:

density is in grams per cubic centimetre (g/cm^3) or kilograms per cubic metre (kg/m^3)

mass is in grams (g) or kilograms (kg)

volume is in cubic centimetres (cm^3) or cubic metres (m^3)

Example 1: Finding the volume of a regular shape

A gold bar measures 12 cm × 5 cm × 4 cm and has a mass of 4632 g.

What is the density of gold?

First find the volume of the gold bar:

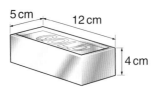

$$\text{Volume} = \text{length} \times \text{width} \times \text{height}$$

$$= 12 \times 5 \times 4$$

$$= 240 \text{ cm}^3$$

Now use the equation to calculate the density of the gold.

$$\text{Density} = \frac{\text{mass}}{\text{volume}}$$

$$\text{Density} = \frac{4632 \text{ g}}{240 \text{ cm}^3}$$

$$\text{Density} = 19.3 \text{ g/cm}^3$$

Repeat the calculation taking the mass of gold as 4.632 kg.

Check your units for the density of the gold.

Example 2: Measuring volume by displacement

As we saw above, the volume of a regular object, like a cube, can be found by doing a little calculation. However, to find the volume of an irregularly shaped object, you can use the displacement of water in a measuring cylinder.

The diagram shows how to measure the volume of a small stone.

The measurements are:

Volume of water with small stone added = 75 cm³

Volume of water at the start = 60 cm³

Therefore, volume of small stone = 15 cm³

This stone weighed 30 grams. What was its density?

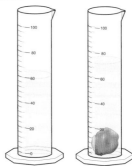

$$\text{Density} = \frac{\text{mass}}{\text{volume}}$$

$$\text{Density} = \frac{30 \text{ g}}{15 \text{ cm}^3}$$

$$\text{Density} = 2 \text{ g/cm}^3$$

Investigation: Measuring the density of water

The aim of this investigation is to find the density of water. You will need:

- A clean, dry measuring cylinder – 100 cm³ or 250 cm³ is ideal.
- An electronic balance (weighing machine).

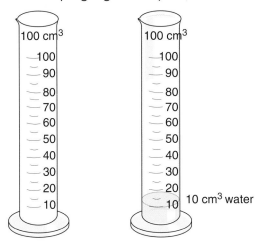

Measure the mass of the measuring cylinder (M1) in grams, as accurately as the balance will allow.

Remove the measuring cylinder from the balance and add water carefully up to the 10 cm³ line.

Reweigh the measuring cylinder (M2). The mass of water added will be (M2 – M1). Record the mass and the volume of water added.

Repeat the procedure, adding 10 cm³ of water at a time.

Note: It may be possible to measure the mass of the water directly if the weighing machine is tared (set to zero) when the empty measuring cylinder is weighed. If a 250 cm³ measuring cylinder is used, it will be easier to add the water in 25 cm³ lots.

1 (a) Draw a graph of volume of liquid (x axis) against mass of liquid
         (y axis). Draw a straight 'line of best fit' through the data and the origin.
   (b) Write out the relationship between mass, volume and density.
   (c) Use your graph to calculate the density of water. Explain how the
         graph provides you with this information.

Investigation: Measuring the density of air

The aim of this investigation is to find the density of air. You will need:

- a large balloon
- a bucket or container large enough to fully immerse the inflated balloon
- an electronic balance (weighing machine), sensitive to 0.1 g
- a measuring jug or large cylinder.

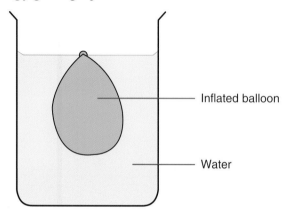

Inflated balloon

Water

Measure the mass of the empty balloon (M1) in grams.

Inflate the balloon.

Immerse the balloon in the water – the water must completely cover the balloon, but not your hands!

Note the water level in the container – mark it with a marker pen.

Take the balloon out and leave it to dry.

Pour water from the jug or cylinder into the container until the water level matches the level with the immersed balloon. The volume of water used (V cm³) is equal to the volume of the balloon.

Check that the balloon is completely dry and then measure the mass of the inflated balloon (M2).

1 (a) Calculate the mass of air in the inflated balloon
  (b) Calculate the density of air in g/cm³.
  (c) Compare your results with other members of your class or group. Write down your findings.
2 Your measurements will have demonstrated that air has mass. Explain why you would expect this to be true.

Exercise 6.1: Density

1 This diagram shows a block of aluminium that has a mass of 270 g.
   Calculate the density of the block. State the formula you use and show
   your working.

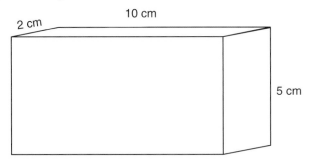

2 The density of a substance can be measured in g/cm³.
   (a) If 10 litres (10 000 cm³) of a liquid has a mass of 975 g, what is its density?
   (b) A metal has a density of 9.0 g/cm³. What is the mass of a cube of this
      metal that has sides that are 3 cm long?
   (c) If a salt solution has a density of 1.2 g/cm³, what volume of the solution
      would have a mass of 840 g?

7 Vibration, waves and sound

◯ What are waves?

Waves are a way of moving energy from one place to another. No matter is transferred when this energy is moved.

Did you know?

Waves can be observed on the surface of water, for example when a drop of water hits the surface of a puddle or when you drop a stone into a pond.

Any disturbance can cause a wave. As well as dropping stones into water, you can see a wave by flicking a rope or by vibrating a spring, such as a slinky spring.

If you shake one end of a slinky spring from side to side you will see waves travelling through it.

■ Ripples on a pond's surface. The waves spread out from the point where the drop of water hits the surface, carrying energy to all parts of the pond. However, the water itself does *not* move from the middle of the pond to the edges.

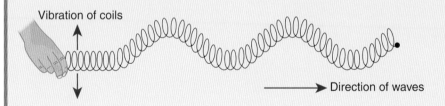

Vibration of coils

Direction of waves

Describing a wave

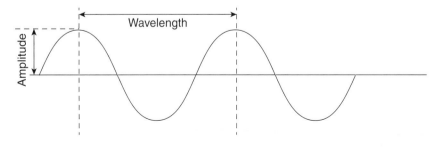

Wavelength

Amplitude

- The **amplitude** of the wave is the maximum vertical disturbance caused by the wave – in other words, its height.
- The **wavelength** is the distance between the corresponding points on two consecutive disturbances (often shown as the distance between two successive peaks).
- The **frequency** is the number of waves produced (or passing one particular point) in one second.

You will find out more about frequency, wavelength and amplitude in the section on 'different sounds', later in this chapter.

Preliminary knowledge: Vibration and sound

There are many different sounds but, as you know, they all have one thing in common. Sounds only happen when something **vibrates**. When something vibrates to make a sound, it moves backwards and forwards. Sometimes it is really easy to see a **vibration**, but at other times we can *hear* a sound without *seeing* a vibration. Even if we can't see a vibration, one *must* be happening if we hear a sound. We can sometimes demonstrate a vibration even if we can't see one.

■ Sound depends on vibrations. Some vibrations are invisible. The sound from a drum comes from the vibration of the drum skin. Some vibrations are more obvious. You can see the movement of the guitar strings as the music is played.

Did you know?

A tuning fork is used by musicians when they are tuning their instruments. You can show the invisible vibrations of a tuning fork by tapping it and then pushing it into a beaker of water.

The fork makes the water vibrate enough for us to see it!

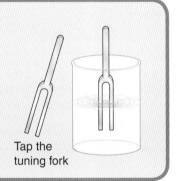

Tap the tuning fork

Everyday sounds

Many of the sounds we hear every day come from radios, MP3 players or televisions. These work by making a **loudspeaker** (speaker) vibrate.

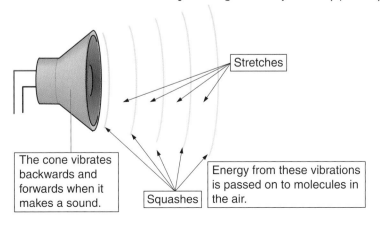

Stretches

The cone vibrates backwards and forwards when it makes a sound.

Squashes

Energy from these vibrations is passed on to molecules in the air.

Did you know?

You can see flour or talcum powder moving about on an old loudspeaker cone when it is switched on. Don't try this on new speakers – it makes a mess!

Sound travels as waves

Sound energy travels because it is passed on from molecule to molecule in the air, between the source of sound and our ears. The molecules move backwards and forwards in a pattern we call a **sound wave**. The pattern looks as if some molecules are pushed together: these parts of the wave are called compressions; others are more spread out: these parts are rarefactions. Here is a diagram showing this pattern:

> **Quieter sounds**: the sound is quieter the further away you are from the source because energy is lost, so particles vibrate less.

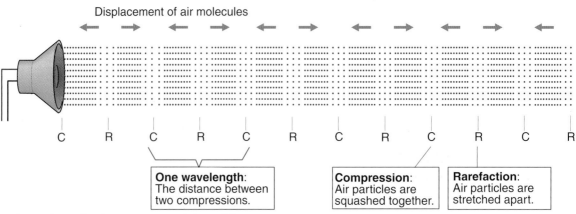

Direction of sound wave ⟹

Displacement of air molecules

C R C R C R C R C R C R

One wavelength: The distance between two compressions.

Compression: Air particles are squashed together.

Rarefaction: Air particles are stretched apart.

■ A sound wave involves movement of air particles

Sound and echoes

Sound waves can be **reflected** from a boundary in the same way as all waves, including light rays.

If you make a sound such as a shout or a bang near a cliff or a big building, you may hear an echo. This is caused by the sound waves bouncing back to you.

The second sound is heard after the first sound because of the time required for the sound to travel to and from the building (wall).

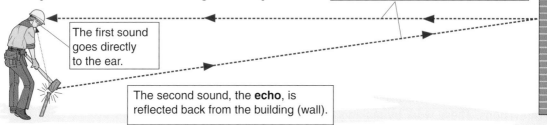

The first sound goes directly to the ear.

The second sound, the **echo**, is reflected back from the building (wall).

Sound waves and echoes can be used to locate underwater objects. A ship on the surface sends out a sound wave and then picks up the echo from anything beneath the ship. This technique, shown on the next page, is called **echo-sounding** or **sonar**. Echo-sounding can be used:

- to locate sunken ships
- to detect submarines
- to search for shoals of fish
- to check that the water is deep enough for a ship to move safely in shallow water.

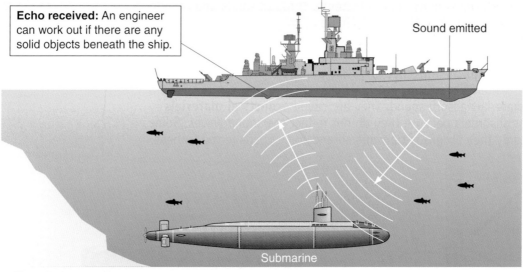

Echo received: An engineer can work out if there are any solid objects beneath the ship.

Sound emitted

Submarine

■ Uses of echo-sounding

Sound needs a material to travel through

Sound waves must have something to pass through, or they can't travel from one place to another. Most of the sounds we hear travel through the air, but sound can also travel through other materials. These materials include liquids, such as water, and solids, such as brick, wood and glass.

Sound travels through the Earth ...
An earthquake in one part of the world sends vibrations to other parts of the Earth. Scientists can use special instruments to listen to these vibrations.

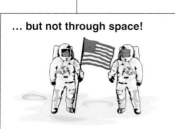

... but not through space!

There are no particles in space, so vibrations cannot be passed on. Astronauts need mobile phones to speak to one other.

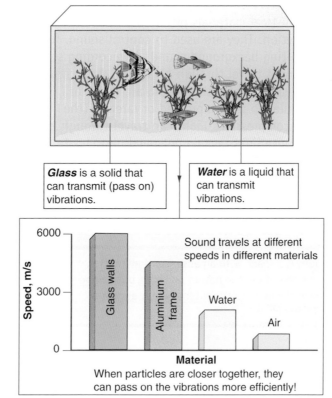

Glass is a solid that can transmit (pass on) vibrations.

Water is a liquid that can transmit vibrations.

Sound travels at different speeds in different materials

Speed, m/s

Glass walls

Aluminium frame

Water

Air

Material
When particles are closer together, they can pass on the vibrations more efficiently!

■ Sounds are transmitted through solid, liquid and gas

Sound waves travel much more efficiently through solids and liquids than through the air. You can check this by listening to a gentle tap on a laboratory bench – try it. You can hear it if your ear is pressed close to the bench but you may not hear it at all if you rely on it travelling through the air. Anything that the sound energy can travel through is called a medium.

Some materials absorb sound. They are called **acoustical materials** and act as absorbers because they do not reflect the sound waves. Some of the energy they absorb is transmitted and some is converted to heat.

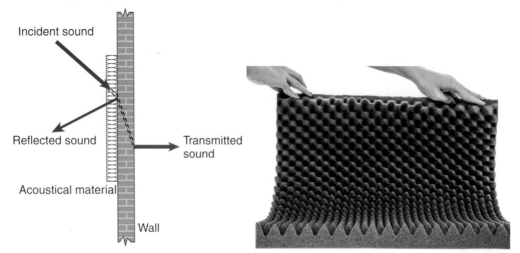

These acoustical materials often have soft, curved surfaces to reduce reflection. They are used to control sound, for example limiting background sounds in recording studios.

Sound cannot travel through a vacuum. A vacuum is an empty space where there is no air, water or other molecules to be compressed or rarefied (the opposite of compressed). Light can travel through a vacuum because light rays do not need particles to pass on their energy.

The need for a medium can be shown using a vacuum bell:

As air is drawn out, the ringing sound becomes quieter and quieter – but you can still see the clanger moving!

A vacuum is a space with an absence of all matter. Vacuums do not exist in nature on Earth, but can be created in the laboratory. Outer space is almost a perfect vacuum.

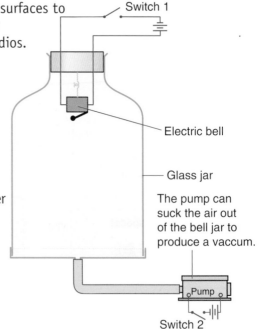

7 Vibration, waves and sound

The speed of sound

Sound travels much more slowly than light. This makes it much easier to measure the speed of sound than the speed of light. These measurements can be made outdoors using echo timing, or indoors using time switches and an electronic timer.

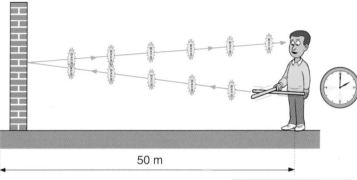

50 m

- Bang a stick and listen for the echo. The sound has travelled 100 m.
- Bang the stick in a rhythm, so the next bang exactly coincides with the echo.
- Another person uses a stop watch to time one hundred bangs.

So

$$\text{Speed of sound} = \frac{\text{distance}}{\text{time}} = \frac{100 \times 100}{\text{time taken}}$$

> The speed of sound is 330 metres per second. Light travels at 300 million metres per second. You will not be expected to memorise these values, only to have an understanding of the comparison between the two – light travels much faster than sound!

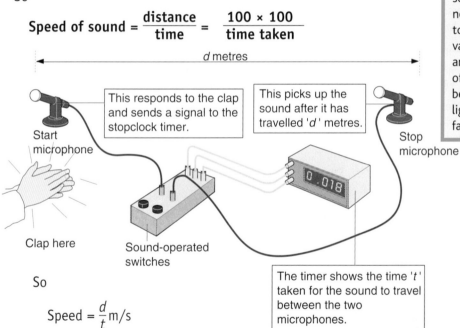

d metres

Start microphone

This responds to the clap and sends a signal to the stopclock timer.

This picks up the sound after it has travelled '*d*' metres.

Stop microphone

0.018

Clap here

Sound-operated switches

The timer shows the time '*t*' taken for the sound to travel between the two microphones.

So

$$\text{Speed} = \frac{d}{t}\,\text{m/s}$$

Light travels faster than sound

Because light travels so much more quickly than sound, we can see an event happen before we hear it. A well-known example of this difference concerns thunder and lightning. During a thunderstorm you usually see the lightning before you hear the thunder. In fact, the light travels so quickly that you see the lightning almost as soon as it happens. The differences between the speed of sound and light means that you can work out how far away the thunderstorm actually is, see the next page.

Thunder (sound) travels 1 km in 3 seconds
Lightning (light) travels 1 000 000 times faster (we see it instantly!)

$$\textbf{Distance from storm} = \frac{\textbf{time between lightning and thunder}}{\textbf{3}}$$

For example, if you **hear** thunder 9 seconds after you see lightning, the storm is $\frac{9}{3}$ = 3 kilometres away.

Another example that illustrates the difference between the speeds of sound and light is when you see the smoke from an explosion before you hear the bang.

Exercise 7.1: Sound

1 Complete the sentences using words from this list:
   vibrates   air   liquids   solids
   Sounds are made when something _____ . Vibrations then travel through the _____ to our ears. Vibrations can also travel through _____ (such as water) and _____ (such as brick).

2 Jack throws a stone into a pond. He hears the plop sound and watches ripples spreading out across the surface of the pond. Which travels fastest: sound, ripples on water or light?

3 Which of these sentences about sound is correct?
   (a) Sound cannot travel through air.
   (b) Sound only travels through air.
   (c) Sound cannot travel through a vacuum.
   (d) Sound cannot travel through water.
   (e) Sound travels well through space.

4 Look at the diagram of the vacuum bell (page 90).
   (a) Say what you would hear when switch 1 is closed.
   (b) What would you hear when the pump is switched on? Give reasons for your answers.

Working Scientifically

Different sounds

You have learned that sounds can only happen if an object vibrates and that sound travels as waves.

Not all sounds are the same. Some sounds are louder than others, and some sounds are higher (squeakier) than others. It is useful to look at the pattern of vibrations in a particular sound to try to understand why sounds are so different.

Looking at sound

A microphone is able to change the vibrations in the air into electrical signals. The vibrations in the air cause the diaphragm (a thin layer of material held taut) in the

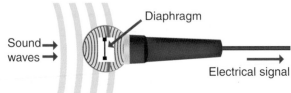

Diaphragm
Sound →
waves →
Electrical signal

microphone to vibrate. The diaphragm vibrations are converted into an electrical signal.

These signals can be seen as a wave pattern if the microphone is connected to an instrument called an **oscilloscope**. This wave pattern is called a trace. The trace shows the changes in pressure of the air as it hits the microphone.

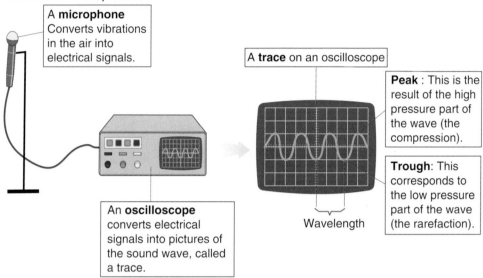

A **microphone**
Converts vibrations in the air into electrical signals.

A **trace** on an oscilloscope

Peak : This is the result of the high pressure part of the wave (the compression).

Trough: This corresponds to the low pressure part of the wave (the rarefaction).

Wavelength

An **oscilloscope** converts electrical signals into pictures of the sound wave, called a trace.

Amplitude and the loudness of sounds

All sounds are caused by vibrations. Sometimes these vibrations are too small to see (see the beginning of this chapter) but sometimes they can be seen quite easily. If you started to play a guitar, you would be able to see the string vibrate as it makes a sound. You could make the sound **louder** if the string were plucked so hard that the vibrations were very large. The sound would be **quieter** (softer) if the string were plucked gently and the vibrations were quite small.

Large vibrations in an object make bigger sound waves. A big sound wave has **more energy** than a small one and this is why it sounds louder. In other words, the harder you hit or pluck something, the more energy there will be in a vibration from this object, and the louder the sound will be.

This is the *amplitude* of the wave. More energy (a louder sound) spreads and compresses particles more. Because of this, *peaks* get *higher* and *troughs* get *lower*.

■ Loudness will depend on energy

The size of the vibrations is called the **amplitude** of the wave. The more energy a wave has, the greater the amplitude.

- A **quiet** noise means there are **small vibrations**, a **small amplitude** and **very little energy**.
- A **loud** noise creates **big vibrations**, **big amplitude** and **a lot of energy**.

Pitch is another difference between sounds

The pitch of a sound is how high or low the sound is. There are several things that affect the pitch of a sound:

- The **size of the object** that is vibrating. For example, in stringed instruments the **longer** the string the **lower** the pitch and the **thicker** the string the **lower** the pitch. Small wind instruments (e.g. a piccolo) make a higher pitched sound than a large one (e.g. a bassoon). A large drum makes a deeper sound (lower pitch) than a small one.

- The **tightness** of the object that is vibrating. For example, in stringed instruments the **tighter** the string the **higher** the pitch.

The pitch of the sound depends on how many vibrations (how many compressions and rarefactions) are fitted into the same amount of time. Scientists can measure how many vibrations take place in a time as short as one second. This is called the **frequency** of the sound. If there is a high frequency, i.e. many vibrations per second, the sound will be very high (squeaky) and if there is a low frequency, i.e. only a few vibrations per second, the sound will be very low (deep). The frequency of a sound is measured in hertz (Hz).

> As the frequency is doubled, the wavelength is halved. A scientist would say that they are **inversely proportional** to each other.

1 Hz = 1 cycle per second

High frequency

Baby   Loudspeaker

Many vibrations in a short time: **high-pitched** sound.

100 Hz note

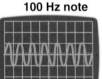

Low frequency

Few vibrations in a short time: **low-pitched** sound.

50 Hz note

Opera singer

Did you know?

Helium gas is much less dense than air. If you breathed in helium, your voice would travel more quickly (with a higher frequency). The sound travels normally as it passes through the air, but the higher frequencies are heard more than normal. The result is a squeaky voice!

Do **not** try this – breathing in helium can be dangerous, even fatal because it reduces the supply of oxygen to the body.

Exercise 7.2: Pitch and loudness

1 Complete the following paragraph, using the words in the list below.

hertz   frequency   wavelength   pitch

The distance between the tops of the waves on an oscilloscope trace is called
the _____ . The number of these that pass per second is called the _____ of
the sound – it is measured in units called _____ and directly affects the _____ of
a sound.

2 Nadia can change the ringtone on her mobile phone. These diagrams show
the patterns made by four sound waves on an oscilloscope screen.

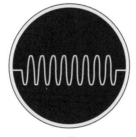
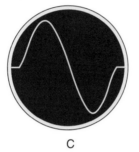

| A | B | C | D |

Which trace matches each of these descriptions?
(a) A loud sound with a high pitch.
(b) A loud sound with a low pitch.
(c) A quiet sound with a high pitch.
(d) Two sounds with the same frequency.
(e) Two sounds with the same amplitude.

3 Imagine you were playing a guitar. How could you alter the instrument so
that it made lower-pitched sounds?

Extension questions

4 Describe a fair test you could carry out to check if the length of a string
affects the pitch of the sound that is made when the string is plucked.
Describe how you could use an oscilloscope to check your results.

Working Scientifically

5 Freddie wanted to check something about the loudness of sounds. He
dropped a number of weights onto the floor, and used a soundmeter to find
out the loudness of the sound. Here are the results of his experiment.

Number of weights	1	15	6	10	10	15	20	22
Loudness of sound (units on sound-meter)	3	3	18	18	29	43	59	65

(a) Plot a graph of his results. Draw a ring around any anomalous results
before drawing the line.
(b) What is the pattern of his results?
(c) Use the graph to estimate the loudness of dropping 12 weights.
(d) Draw the oscilloscope traces he would have seen if he had compared the
effects of five weights and ten weights.
(e) Give two things he had to do if this were a fair test.
(f) Give one way in which he could have improved the experiment.

The ear and hearing

When the cone of a loudspeaker is vibrating, it makes the air next to it vibrate as well. The air is squashed and stretched to make sound waves. These sound waves travel through the air until they reach our ears. When the vibrations reach our ears, they make our eardrums vibrate. These tiny pieces of skin pass on their vibrations through a series of bones to a structure called the cochlea. This structure can change vibrations into electrical messages. These messages are then sent to the brain. When these messages reach the brain, we finally hear a sound.

> **Did you know?**
>
> You don't actually hear a sound until the electrical messages reach the brain.

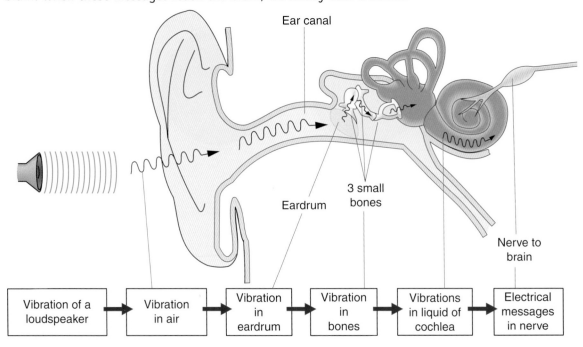

Ear canal

3 small bones

Eardrum

Nerve to brain

| Vibration of a loudspeaker | → | Vibration in air | → | Vibration in eardrum | → | Vibration in bones | → | Vibrations in liquid of cochlea | → | Electrical messages in nerve |

Problems with hearing

Different people can hear different sounds. The **audible range** for a person tells us the upper and lower frequencies of sound that the person can detect. The audible range depends on how well the vibrations in the eardrum are passed on through the tiny bones.

As we get older, these bones wear out and we find it especially difficult to hear high-frequency (high-pitched) sounds. The audible range is reduced as our ears get older!

> **Did you know?**
>
> Some animals can move this part of the ear (called the pinna) so they collect very weak sound waves from all directions.
>
>

The ears can suffer more serious damage than this general wear-and-tear and we can become deaf. This deafness can be temporary or permanent, depending on what causes it. These are some of the problems associated with hearing:

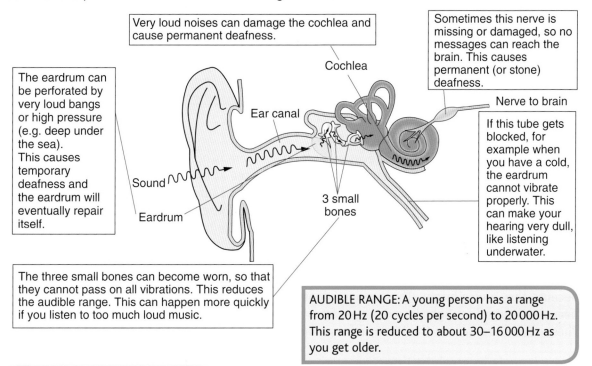

Very loud noises can damage the cochlea and cause permanent deafness.

Sometimes this nerve is missing or damaged, so no messages can reach the brain. This causes permanent (or stone) deafness.

Cochlea

Nerve to brain

The eardrum can be perforated by very loud bangs or high pressure (e.g. deep under the sea).
This causes temporary deafness and the eardrum will eventually repair itself.

Ear canal

If this tube gets blocked, for example when you have a cold, the eardrum cannot vibrate properly. This can make your hearing very dull, like listening underwater.

Sound

Eardrum

3 small bones

The three small bones can become worn, so that they cannot pass on all vibrations. This reduces the audible range. This can happen more quickly if you listen to too much loud music.

AUDIBLE RANGE: A young person has a range from 20 Hz (20 cycles per second) to 20 000 Hz. This range is reduced to about 30–16 000 Hz as you get older.

Exercise 7.3: Hearing

1 Complete the sentences using words from the list:
waves   brain   hear   cochlea   bones   eardrums
Sound _____ travel through the air until they reach our ears. When the vibrations reach our ears they make our _____ vibrate. These pass on the vibrations through a series of _____ to a structure called the _____ , which changes vibrations into electrical messages and sends them to the _____ , which is when we finally _____ a sound.

Extension questions

2 Design an experiment to find out who has the most sensitive hearing in your group. Say exactly what you will measure and explain how you would make certain that your experiment was a fair test.

Working Scientifically

3 Use a library book or the internet to find out how a hearing-aid works. Display your findings as a poster.

8 Light waves

Light

Preliminary knowledge: Light sources

Light is a sort of energy that your eyes can detect. If there is no light, in other words, when it is completely dark, you cannot see at all. The light we need in order to see objects comes from **light sources** including the Sun, stars, light bulbs and burning objects. These objects or light sources are able to produce light energy, for example by burning, or by the conversion of electrical energy. Anything that can produce and give off its own light energy is called a luminous source.

Some other objects look as though they are light sources because they are so bright. These objects look bright to us because they reflect light into our eyes from another light source. These reflectors include the Moon, mirrors and even this page.

Light travels in straight lines

Light is made of rays that always travel in straight lines. This means that we can't see an object if there is anything in the way of these straight lines. When we try to draw the way light is travelling, we always use straight lines.

Sun

Car headlamps

■ Luminous sources give out light

The Moon reflects light from the sun.

THIS WRITING

You can read this because light is reflected off the paper.

■ These objects are not luminous even though we can see them

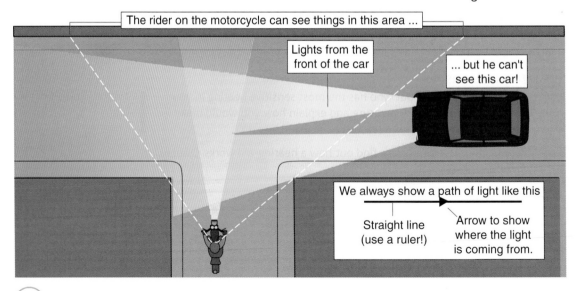

The rider on the motorcycle can see things in this area ...

Lights from the front of the car

... but he can't see this car!

We always show a path of light like this

Straight line (use a ruler!)

Arrow to show where the light is coming from.

Preliminary knowledge: Shadows

Light can pass through some but not through all materials. If
something gets in the way of light, a shadow is formed.

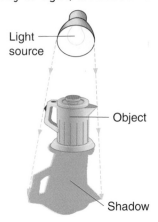

Light — source

— Object

Shadow

■ Light cannot get around an
object, so it produces a shadow

Light can pass through *some* materials

Transparent materials are materials that light can pass straight
through. We say the light is **transmitted** through the material. The
light (energy) isn't scattered or absorbed when it passes through the
material. This means that you can clearly see objects that are behind
these materials or inside boxes made of these materials. Transparent
materials include glass, clear plastic/Perspex and water.

Light can
pass through
a transparent
material,
which means
that objects
can be seen
very clearly

Light rays pass
straight through a
transparent material.

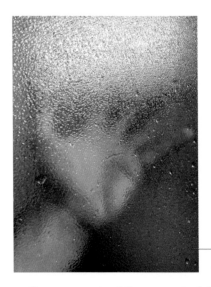

Translucent materials allow light to pass through (transmission), but they change some of the light rays, absorbing light energy and re-emitting it in all directions. This is called **diffuse scattering**. It means that you can't get a clear picture of an object if it is behind a translucent material. Translucent materials include some plastic, tissue paper and frosted glass.

> Some light can pass through, but objects are not seen clearly.

> Light rays are all mixed up when they pass through a translucent material.

Opaque materials are materials that stop all light from passing through. This means that none of the light rays can get from one side of the material to the other. You can't see an object through an opaque material. Opaque materials include wood, metal, brick and cloth.

> No light can pass through an opaque material. You cannot see what is inside this box!

When light rays from a source are blocked, a **shadow** is formed. This can be shown by carefully drawing a diagram of how light rays fall on an opaque material.

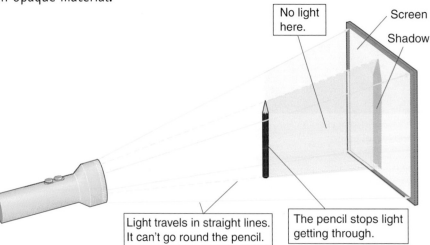

> No light here.

Screen

Shadow

> Light travels in straight lines. It can't go round the pencil.

> The pencil stops light getting through.

Two things affect the way shadows are made:

- Shadows are **larger** if the object is close to the light source
- Shadows are **shorter** if the light source is almost overhead.

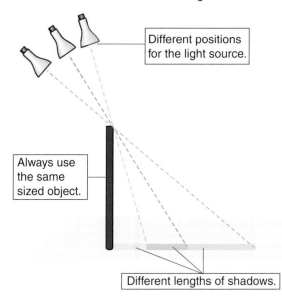

Different positions for the light source.

Always use the same sized object.

Different lengths of shadows.

You can study each of these effects by carrying out **fair tests**.

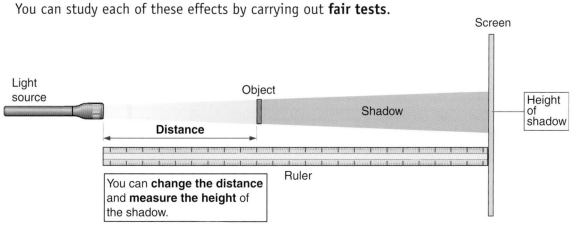

Screen

Light source

Object

Shadow

Height of shadow

Distance

Ruler

You can **change the distance** and **measure the height** of the shadow.

Exercise 8.1: Shadows

1 (a) Give an example of a transparent material.
  (b) Say what it might be used for and why.

2 (a) Give an example of a translucent material.
  (b) Say what it might be used for and why.

3 (a) Give an example of an opaque material.
  (b) Say what it might be used for and why.

4 Draw a diagram to show how a shadow forms behind a garden fence on a sunny day. Use a ruler to draw straight lines.

Extension questions

5 Copy this diagram exactly. Carefully draw light rays to show how a shadow forms on the screen. Measure the height of the shadow.

Object

Light source

6 Samantha decided to carry out an experiment on shadows. She changed the distance between the light source and the object, and then measured the height of the shadow on the screen. Here are her results.

Working Scientifically

Distance between light source and object, in millimetres	Height of shadow, in millimetres
20	90
40	60
60	30
80	15
100	9
120	6

(a) Draw a graph of the results.
(b) What is the pattern of these results?
(c) How big would the shadow be if the light source was 50 mm from the object?

○ The speed of light

In Chapter 7 you learned about the speed of sound. **Light travels very fast**, at a definite speed in an unchanging medium, which is about a million times faster than sound. At this speed light crosses a room, where air is the medium, in less than 1 millionth of a second.

Light can travel through a vacuum. (Remember that sound cannot.)

The jet plane travels at about 400 m per second.

The light from these headlights travels at 300 000 000 m per second.

This Formula 1 racing car travels at around 1/15th km per second.

It is very difficult to measure the speed of light, but scientists have found that light travels at an ultimate speed of about 300 000 000 metres per second (300 000 km per second) in a vacuum. This is about a million times faster than the speed of an aeroplane. You will not be expected to memorise this value – only to have an appreciation for how very fast light travels.

How we see things

Preliminary knowledge: Eyes

We see things when **light enters our eyes**. The light can come:

- directly from the source to our eyes, for example light from a burning match
- when light from a source is reflected from (in other words, bounces off) an object.

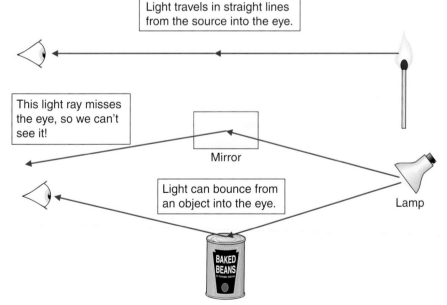

Light travels in straight lines from the source into the eye.

This light ray misses the eye, so we can't see it!

Mirror

Light can bounce from an object into the eye.

Lamp

BAKED BEANS

No matter where the light comes from, we just won't see an object unless:

- the light can reach the eye in a straight line from the object
- the light rays can actually enter the eye.

The pinhole camera

A **pinhole camera** is a very simple device that can show how light travels in straight lines and can form an image on a screen. The image that is formed is *inverted* (upside down). This is how an image is formed on the back of a human eye. Our brain has learned that the image needs to be corrected, so that we actually see things the right way up.

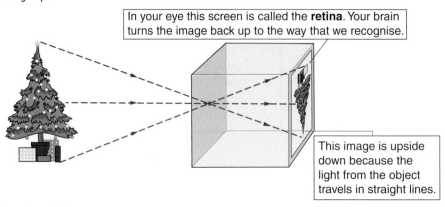

In your eye this screen is called the **retina**. Your brain turns the image back up to the way that we recognise.

This image is upside down because the light from the object travels in straight lines.

Exercise 8.2: Light

1 Complete this paragraph using the words from the list below:

light　　　　reflect　　　　luminous
shadow　　　　energy　　　　straight lines

You can't see an object unless there is some _____ . The objects you can see are either _____ (give out light) or _____ light into your eyes. Light is a form of _____ and always travels in _____ _____ . A _____ is formed because light cannot pass through solid objects.

2 Which of these objects are light sources?
Moon　　Sun　　a torch　　a burning candle
the silver paper wrapper from a chocolate bar
the chrome radiator grille on a sports car

3 During a power cut, electric lights go off. Write down three different things you could use to provide you with light during a power cut.

Extension questions

4 Draw a diagram to explain why you can see your watch by moonlight. It isn't a luminous watch!

5 Use straight lines to explain why you can still see a cat in the shadow behind a house. This is definitely not a luminous cat!

6 Use the internet or your library to find out how scientists are able to measure the speed of light.

Mirrors and the reflection of light

You have now learned that some objects are luminous – we can see them because they give out their own light.

We can see other objects because they reflect the light that shines on them.

Remember that light rays travel in straight lines.

Mirrors reflect light

You should already know quite a lot about mirrors, but here is a little revision before we look at them in more detail. When light hits a shiny surface, the light rays bounce off the surface. We say that the light rays are **reflected**. If the reflection gives a perfect image, the surface is acting as a mirror.

We can use almost any shiny surface to act like a mirror. Dull or rough surfaces are no use as mirrors because they don't let the light bounce back without mixing up the light rays. There are many other surfaces that do reflect light but don't act as mirrors. Paper is a very good example of this kind of material.

Lamp

Light bounces off the smooth surface – it is reflected.
A smooth, shiny surface reflects all the light falling on it.

A mirror is drawn with the shaded side at the back.

Mirror

A smooth sea looks bright and the colour of the sky. The small waves act like moving mirrors and the sun's reflections seem to sparkle. Bigger, broken waves make the sea look darker and duller.

Lamp

Very small bumps mean the light rays are reflected in many different directions. This means we can see what's written on the paper from more than one direction.

Paper

We can see words on the paper from anywhere over here.

Lamp

Light rays get so mixed up that we don't get a clear reflection from a very rough surface.

Cloth

■ Reflection from different surfaces

Looking in a mirror

A mirror that is flat is called a plane mirror. When you look into a plane mirror, you see that:

- the image you see is *the same size* as the object that is reflected
- the image is the *right way up* (**upright**)
- the image seems to be *behind* the mirror (**virtual image**, see later)
- the images are *back-to-front* or *reversed* (**laterally inverted**). This means that you would see any writing back-to-front, and so it would be difficult to read!

Sometimes it's really important that you are able to read a word in a mirror. If an ambulance or a fire engine drives up behind your car, you need to know exactly what it is. Because of the need to do this the words 'AMBULANCE' or 'FIRE ENGINE' are painted back to front on the front of these vehicles. This means a car driver will see the words the right way round in the car's rear-view mirror.

This is what the front of a fire engine looks like.

This is how it looks in the rear-view mirror of a car.

Investigation: Rules of reflection

The aim of this experiment is to investigate the way light behaves when it hits a reflective surface.

We can study reflection using this apparatus:

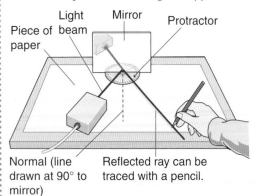

Light beam, Mirror, Protractor, Piece of paper

Normal (line drawn at 90° to mirror)

Reflected ray can be traced with a pencil.

- Plug the raybox into a power pack, taking care to use the correct voltage (your teacher will explain).
- Stand your mirror on the line at the bottom of the protractor. Draw on the normal line.
- Send a ray of light to the mirror so that it hits at the centre of the protractor. These rays are called **incident rays**. Measure the angle between the incident ray and the normal using the protractor. Write down this angle. This is called the angle of incidence.
- Look carefully at the **reflected ray** and measure the angle at which the light is reflected (the angle between the reflected ray and the normal). Write down this angle. This is the angle of reflection.
- Try this several times for different angles of incidence.
- Copy the diagram below and draw in the reflected ray to show the angle of reflection.

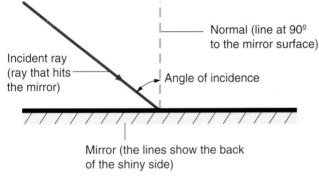

Normal (line at 90° to the mirror surface)

Incident ray (ray that hits the mirror)

Angle of incidence

Mirror (the lines show the back of the shiny side)

1 What conclusion can you reach about the angle of reflection?

No matter where we move the raybox to, the angle of reflection and the angle of incidence are always the same, so remember:

angle of incidence (i) = angle of reflection (r)

Using a periscope

The direction of light rays can be changed more than once by using more than one mirror. A **periscope** uses two mirrors to let you see round or over an object. Periscopes were first used by soldiers in the First World War – they let soldiers see out of their trenches without the risk of being shot. They also let the commander of a submarine see what is going on at the surface of the water, or allow the driver of a school bus to see what's going on upstairs.

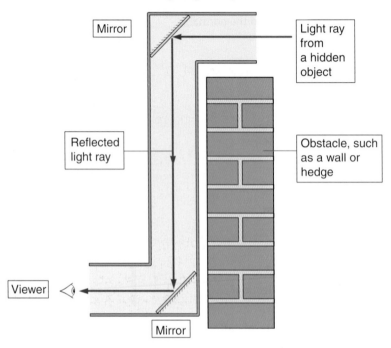

Mirror

Light ray from a hidden object

Reflected light ray

Obstacle, such as a wall or hedge

Viewer

Mirror

Seeing around awkward corners: Optical fibres

Optical fibres are made from materials that let light pass along them. They work because light is reflected inside them until it reaches the other end. Optical fibres have many uses:

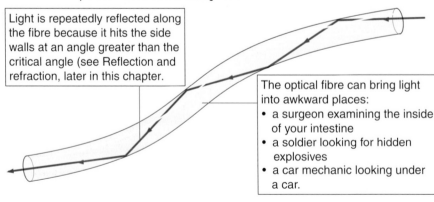

Light is repeatedly reflected along the fibre because it hits the side walls at an angle greater than the critical angle (see Reflection and refraction, later in this chapter.

The optical fibre can bring light into awkward places:
- a surgeon examining the inside of your intestine
- a soldier looking for hidden explosives
- a car mechanic looking under a car.

Exercise 8.3: Reflection

1 (a) Look at the clock, opposite. It is viewed in a mirror. What time is it?
  (b) Write out the same time as it would appear on a *digital* watch viewed in a mirror.

2 Write your name and address (include the postcode) on a piece of paper so that it will be the right way round when viewed in a mirror.

3 What does each of these words mean?
  (a) image   (b) virtual   (c) inverted   (d) plane   (e) incidence

4 Draw a diagram to show how a shopkeeper could use a periscope to keep watch on the goods in another aisle.

Extension questions

5 Make a list of five reflecting surfaces in your home. Choose one of these surfaces that is normally transparent but can sometimes be reflecting (think carefully).

6 Use the Internet or your library to find out how optical cables are used in communications. Try to find out the advantages of using optical cables compared with copper cables.

Refraction of light

Refraction occurs whenever light passes from one substance to another. It happens because of the different speeds at which light is able to pass through different substances. Light passes easily through gases, such as the air, but travels more slowly through materials, such as glass, Perspex or water. It is rather like a car moving at different speeds on different surfaces.

■ Working Scientifically

■ You can demonstrate refraction very simply by placing a straw in a glass of water. It appears to exit the water at a different place to its position under water.

■ Working Scientifically

Investigation: The effects of refraction

The aim of this experiment is to investigate the effects of refraction.

To find out what refraction is, set up the apparatus as shown below:

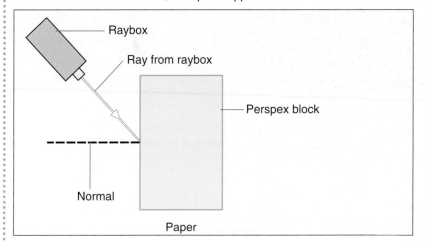

Before you use the raybox, draw around the perspex block and draw in a normal ray (as shown in the diagram above).

Now send a ray along to hit the block at the point where you have drawn the normal ray.

Show the path that the light ray has taken. You can do this by using sharp pencil dots. Use two dots (far apart) to show where the light went on its way to the block; use a dot to show where it left the block, and then use a final dot to mark the emerging ray a long way from the block.

Remove the block and switch off the raybox.

Use a ruler to join the dots and draw in the path of the ray:

- on its way to the block
- through the block
- when it has left the block.

1 (a) Draw what you have found copying the diagram above.
  (b) Use the information that is in your diagram to make the following paragraph correct:
      When a ray of light crosses a boundary into a denser medium (such as going into glass or water from air) it bends **towards/away from** the normal. When light rays pass into a less dense medium (when they go back into air) then they bend **towards/away from** the normal.

Refraction is like the movement of a racing car from tarmac through gravel back to tarmac. One wheel of the racing car is on gravel (like light inside the glass or water) where it moves more slowly, whilst the other is on tarmac (like light in the air) where it can still move quickly. There are two important rules to remember:

- Light rays passing from a **less** dense medium to a **more** dense medium always **bend towards the normal.** The normal is at right angles to the boundary between the two media.
- Light rays passing from a **more** dense to a **less** dense medium always **bend away from the normal.**

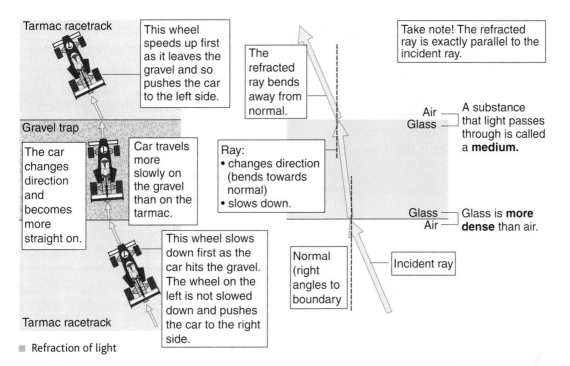

Tarmac racetrack

This wheel speeds up first as it leaves the gravel and so pushes the car to the left side.

Gravel trap

The car changes direction and becomes more straight on.

Car travels more slowly on the gravel than on the tarmac.

This wheel slows down first as the car hits the gravel. The wheel on the left is not slowed down and pushes the car to the right side.

Tarmac racetrack

The refracted ray bends away from normal.

Ray:
• changes direction (bends towards normal)
• slows down.

Normal (right angles to boundary)

Take note! The refracted ray is exactly parallel to the incident ray.

Air
Glass

A substance that light passes through is called a **medium.**

Glass
Air

Glass is **more dense** than air.

Incident ray

■ Refraction of light

Straight on

If both wheels of a racing car hit a sand trap at exactly the same time, they slow down together. The car then continues to go through the sand trap without turning, but it now travels more slowly than it did on the tarmac. Light rays do exactly the same if they pass from one medium to another at right angles.

> Remember: the refracted ray emerging from the block is always exactly parallel to the incident ray.

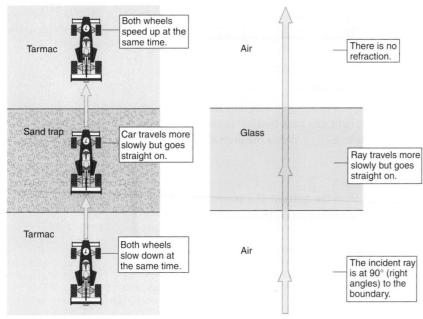

Tarmac

Both wheels speed up at the same time.

Sand trap

Car travels more slowly but goes straight on.

Tarmac

Both wheels slow down at the same time.

Air

There is no refraction.

Glass

Ray travels more slowly but goes straight on.

Air

The incident ray is at 90° (right angles) to the boundary.

■ Light can travel straight through a boundary

Effects of refraction

Refraction can explain some strange effects that you may well have noticed. If you stand in shallow water, your feet seem closer to the surface than they actually are. In the same way, a fish swimming in a stream always seems to be closer to the surface than it is. This can make it hard to catch tiny fish with a net.

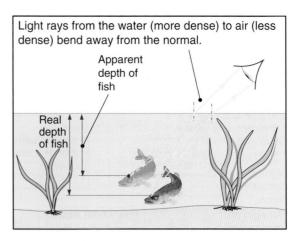

Light rays from the water (more dense) to air (less dense) bend away from the normal.

Apparent depth of fish

Real depth of fish

The **archer fish** has two parts to its eye – the top sees in air … and the bottom part sees in water. This lets the archer fish catch insects from above the surface without worrying about refraction!

Jet of water

Here's an experiment.
- Put a coin in a cup.
- Add some water to level A.
- You can't see the coin.
- Tell your audience that you'll make the coin appear.
- Add more water to level B and HEY PRESTO!

B
A

■ Real and apparent depth

Exercise 8.4: Refraction

1 Complete this paragraph, using words from the list below:

less   away from   medium   refracted

Light is _____ when it reaches a boundary between two different transparent substances. Each of the substances that light can pass through is called a _____ . Light passing from a more dense to a _____ dense medium always bends _____ the normal.

2 Use your knowledge of refraction to explain:
   (a) why it is difficult to pick up a coin from the bottom of a swimming pool
   (b) why it is hard to spear a fish if you are standing on the seashore.
   Use diagrams to help your explanation.

Working Scientifically

Extension question

3 Use a textbook or the internet to find a diagram of a microscope. Make a simple copy of the diagram to show how lenses direct a beam of light through the instrument.

Light, energy and colour

Sound waves can travel only through a definite medium (see Chapter 7) but there is a group of waves, including light, which can travel through a vacuum. These are called **electromagnetic waves** and are produced when molecules, atoms or electrons vibrate when they absorb energy.

There are different types of electromagnetic wave. The type of wave depends on the **frequency** and on the **wavelength** (see Chapter 7). All types of wave travel at the same speed, about 300 000 km per second. This is usually called the **speed of light** because light is a type of electromagnetic wave. The complete range of electromagnetic waves is called the electromagnetic spectrum, and an example is shown here.

> When wavelengths get **shorter**, frequency gets **higher**: scientists say that frequency and wavelength are **inversely proportional** to each other.

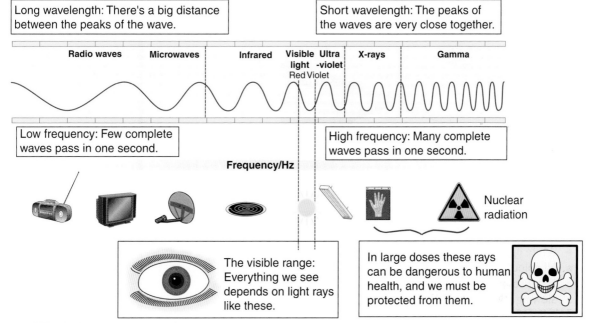

Long wavelength: There's a big distance between the peaks of the wave.

Short wavelength: The peaks of the waves are very close together.

Radio waves   Microwaves   Infrared   Visible light   Ultra-violet   X-rays   Gamma
Red Violet

Low frequency: Few complete waves pass in one second.

High frequency: Many complete waves pass in one second.

Frequency/Hz

Nuclear radiation

The visible range: Everything we see depends on light rays like these.

In large doses these rays can be dangerous to human health, and we must be protected from them.

Visible light

The light that we see is only a small part of the entire electromagnetic spectrum. It is called **visible light** because it can be detected by our eyes. It is also called **white light** because it looks white to our eyes. White light is made up of several different colours. This range of colours is called the visible spectrum. We see the visible spectrum when white light from the Sun hits drops of water. The colours are separated out to produce a rainbow.

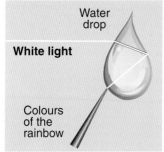

Water drop

White light

Each drop of water splits the white sunlight into a set of different colours.

Colours of the rainbow

> This rhyme can help you remember the seven colours of the rainbow:
>
> Richard of York gave battle in vain.
>
> Red, orange, yellow, green, blue, indigo, violet.

Investigation: Explaining dispersion

The aim of this experiment is to investigate the splitting of white light and making spectra (rainbows).

When light enters a glass block, the rays are refracted (they are bent towards the normal). There is something else that happens that you only really notice with a special shape of block called a prism. It is sometimes called Newton's prism, after Sir Isaac Newton, who created a spectrum in his laboratory using a triangular piece of glass. The angle of the glass in a prism is ideal for splitting white light into its seven different colours.

Shine a white light from a raybox into a prism – set up as in the diagram below. Turn the prism slowly until you see a spectrum of colours as clearly as you can.

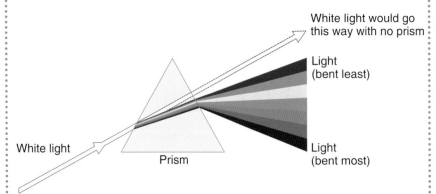

White light would go this way with no prism

Light (bent least)

White light

Prism

Light (bent most)

Let us look at why this happens:

- White light is a mixture of colours.
- All colours are slowed down by the glass.
- Some colours are slowed down more than others.
- Slowing down caused the bending.
1 Complete these sentences:
    (a) _____ is slowed down the most and so is bent the most.
    (b) _____ is slowed down the least and so is bent the least.

Exercise 8.5: Light energy and colour

1 Make up your own rhyme to help you remember the order of colours in the visible spectrum – make this different from the one given in this chapter.

2 Write a short paragraph to explain the appearance of rainbows in the sky or beneath a waterfall.

Extension question

3 When looking at a rainbow, the 'light' seems darker beyond the rainbow. Explain why.

9 Electricity on the move: Electrical circuits

In Chapters 1 and 2 you learned that electricity is a convenient form of energy for human activities. It can move from one place to another through cables or wires and can be changed into other types of energy.

Here we will look at electricity in more detail.

What is electricity?

Electricity can provide the energy to power electrical appliances, but what is it exactly? To get an answer to this, you will need to think back to the structure of the atom (see Chemistry, Chapters 1 and 2). Here's a reminder:

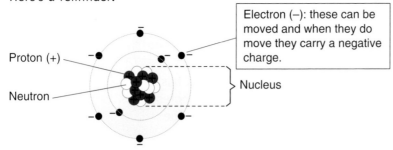

Electron (–): these can be moved and when they do move they carry a negative charge.

Proton (+)

Neutron

Nucleus

Atoms are **neutral** overall; the number of positive charges on protons is balanced by the number of negative charges on electrons.

■ The structure of the atom

Inside the atom there are two types of electric charge: electrons have a **negative** (–) charge and protons have a **positive** (+) charge. Electrons do not always stay attached to atoms. If electrons flow, they set up a current – scientists say that *a current is a flow of charge*.

Round and round: Electrical circuits

You will remember from earlier in your studies of science that blood flows in blood vessels around your body. The blood is pumped from the heart, round the body and then back to the heart. We say it completes a circuit of the body. Electricity flows in a similar sort of way around a circuit.

● Electricity flows through **wires** (also called leads) instead of vessels. These wires act as **electrical conductors** (see Chapter 2).
● Electricity begins and ends a circuit in a **source of energy**, such as a cell (battery).
● Electricity flowing around a circuit is called **electric current**; it is a **flow of charge**.

Whether an electrical appliance uses the mains or a battery, the appliance will not work unless it is part of a **complete circuit.**

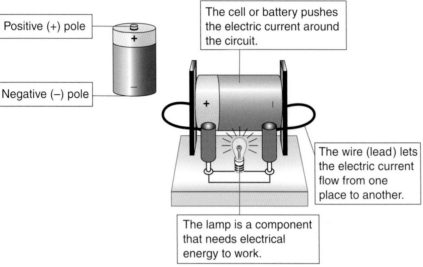

Positive (+) pole

Negative (−) pole

The cell or battery pushes the electric current around the circuit.

The wire (lead) lets the electric current flow from one place to another.

The lamp is a component that needs electrical energy to work.

■ The lamp lights because the circuit is complete

Preliminary knowledge: How to connect up a complete circuit

A cell (battery) pushes electric current around a circuit. Each cell has a **positive** end (+) and a **negative** end (−). These are called the poles or terminals of the cell. The word **polarity** is used when we describe which end of a cell is which and when we look at the direction in which the current is flowing. In order to connect up a complete circuit, you need to:

- attach a lead to the positive pole of the cell
- connect the other end of this lead to a component, such as a bulb. If the component has a positive or negative side, connect the lead to the positive side
- attach another lead from the negative pole of the component to the negative pole of the battery.

There should now be a complete circuit.

....

Investigation: Making electrical circuits

In this experiment you will be making your own electrical circuit.

You will need to assemble a set of electrical circuits. You will need cells, connecting leads, bulbs and a switch.

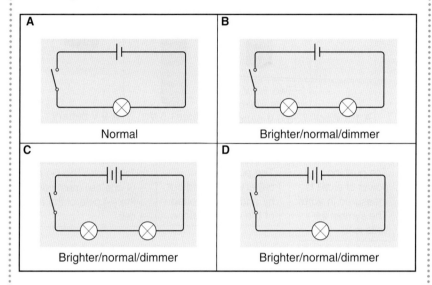

A	B
Normal	Brighter/normal/dimmer
C	D
Brighter/normal/dimmer	Brighter/normal/dimmer

● Make up circuit A. Press the switch and observe the brightness of the bulb.
● Make up the other circuits. When you press the switch, again note the brightness of the bulb. Compare the brightness of B, C and D with that of A. Discuss your results with your teacher.
1 Using circuit A as a control, chose the words below the other circuit diagrams that apply.
2 Explain your observations of bulb brightness as clearly as you can for each of circuits B, C and D. Discuss in terms of current, push of the batteries (cells) and resistance (the difficulty in the circuit).

....

◯ Cells and batteries

A cell is a chemical source of electrical energy. Inside the cell are chemicals and, when these chemicals react together, they make the current flow in a circuit. Once the chemicals have stopped reacting, they cannot react again and the cell stops pushing charge around the circuit.

The 'push' that a cell supplies to move charge around a circuit is measured in volts (V). The higher the voltage of a cell, the more it pushes the charge.

A battery is two or more cells connected together in series (one after another). An electrical appliance, such as a radio, often needs several cells to make it work – this collection of cells is the battery. People often use the word battery when they mean a single cell because it sometimes isn't possible to see all the cells.

Here's a diagram to show you more about cells and batteries:

Positive terminal (+)
(positive pole)

Case

Chemicals
inside cell
(These can
leak out
and damage
electrical
equipment.)

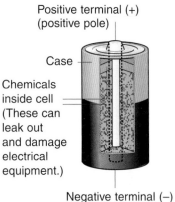

Negative terminal (−)
(negative pole)

A 1.5 V cell

Two 1.5 V
cells make a
3.0 V battery

Three1.5 V
cells make a
4.5 V battery

A 9 V battery
(6 x 1.5 V cells)

The pushing
power of a cell is
measured in **volts**.
The symbol for
volts is V.

The power of a
battery is worked out
by adding the voltage
of the cells together.

Take note: The (+) pole
of one cell must contact
the (−) pole of the next
cell.

■ A 12V battery is used to start a car. It is
made of 8 × 1.5V cells.

Did you know?

You can become a human battery!

- Touch both metal plates at the same time, making
  sure that they are clean first.
- The ammeter shows that a current is flowing.

Copper
plate

Aluminium
plate

Ammeter (see How is
current measured?)

Why does this happen?

Sweat on your hands acts like acid in a battery,
starting chemical reactions with the two metals.
Your hand takes negative charges away from the copper and gives negative
charges to the aluminium. This flow of negative charge produces the current.

It won't hurt – honestly!

Inside a circuit

It can be very difficult to imagine what is going on inside an electrical circuit because we can't actually see anything moving. The flow of electric current around the circuit can be compared again with the flow of blood in the human circulation.

Both electrical circuits and the blood system can have switches to control the flow (see later in this chapter).

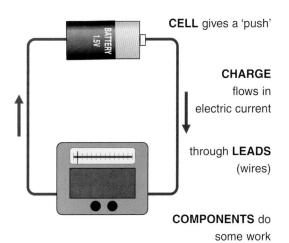

Human circulation

HEART gives a 'push'

BLOOD flows

through **ARTERIES** and **VEINS**

TISSUES and **ORGANS** do some work

Electrical circuit

CELL gives a 'push'

CHARGE flows in electric current

through **LEADS** (wires)

COMPONENTS do some work

A model of electricity

It is sometimes helpful in understanding things we *can't* see to make a model that we *can* see. Imagine a long tube full of small steel balls (ball bearings). Each ball bearing is the same as all the others in the tube and the ball bearings can be pushed through the tube using a handle.

Turning the handle puts energy into this circuit. The energy is transmitted to the paddle wheel by the movement of the ball bearings. The paddle wheel transforms the kinetic energy (energy of movement) of the ball bearings into movement of the paddle wheel.

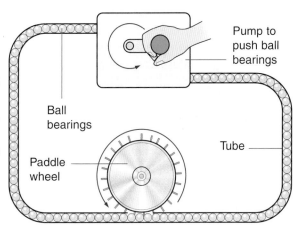

Pump to push ball bearings

Ball bearings

Paddle wheel

Tube

Exercise 9.1: Circuits

1 What three things are needed for a complete circuit?

2 Which type of energy is stored in a cell?

   thermal   kinetic   chemical potential   light

3 What do the following represent in the model of electric current shown above?
   (a) Ball bearings   **(b)** Pump   **(c)** Paddle wheel

❙Working Scientifically

Circuit basics

You have learned that electricity is a flow of charge and that a current can only flow in a complete circuit.

Switches

Switches are used to control the flow of current in an electrical circuit. An *open* switch can put a deliberate break in a circuit. The circuit can be completed again when the switch is *closed*.

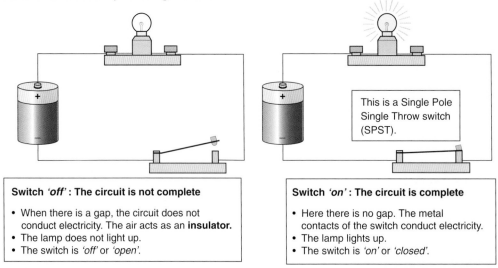

This is a Single Pole Single Throw switch (SPST).

Switch *'off'* : The circuit is not complete

- When there is a gap, the circuit does not conduct electricity. The air acts as an **insulator**.
- The lamp does not light up.
- The switch is *'off'* or *'open'*.

Switch *'on'* : The circuit is complete

- Here there is no gap. The metal contacts of the switch conduct electricity.
- The lamp lights up.
- The switch is *'on'* or *'closed'*.

Preliminary knowledge: Circuit diagrams

A **circuit diagram** is a simple representation of a real circuit that makes circuit drawing easier to master. The diagram should show no breaks or gaps, unless they are put there deliberately with switches. We use circuit symbols to make it easier to draw electrical circuits. Some of these symbols are shown in the table below:

Component	Symbol	What the component is used for
Cell	—┤├—	Provides electrical energy for the circuit
Battery	—┤├┤├—	Provides electrical energy for the circuit
Battery (2+ cells)	—┤├ – – ┤├—	Provides electrical energy for the circuit
Terminals (power supply)	—o o—	Alternative to using cells
Wire (lead) conductor	————	Lets electric current travel through it
Wire conductor crossover	↓	Wire conductor join —•—
Lamp/bulb	—⊗—	Converts electrical energy into thermal and light energy
Motor	—Ⓜ—	Converts electrical energy into movement energy

Component	Symbol	What the component is used for
Buzzer		Converts electrical energy into sound energy
SPST switch (open)		Breaks the circuit and stops the flow of electric current
SPST switch (closed)		Completes the circuit so the electric current can flow
Push button switch		Either completes or breaks a circuit

This diagram shows some examples of using circuit diagrams. You can see that it is easier to work out what is happening by looking at a circuit diagram.

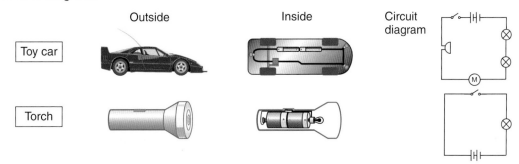

Outside	Inside	Circuit diagram
Toy car		
Torch		

How is current measured?

If there is a light bulb in the circuit, we can judge the size of a current by looking at the **brightness** of the lamp. A large current makes the lamp glow brightly and a small current only makes the lamp glow dimly or not at all.

However, this method is not accurate enough for scientific work, because one person might not agree with another person about what is bright and what isn't. For this reason, an instrument called an ammeter is used to measure the current.

The size of the current is measured in units called amperes (A). Amperes is usually shortened to **amps**.

When an ammeter is used it must be:

- connected **in** the main circuit
- connected with the **red** (+) terminal to the positive terminal on the cell, battery or power supply.

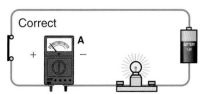

This terminal (the positive terminal) *must* be connected to the positive terminal on the power source.

Here the meter is connected in the circuit.
It measures the current passing through the lamp.

Using an ammeter

Investigation: Measuring current

In this experiment you will be using ammeters to measure the amount of current flowing in a circuit.

You will need a lamp or other electrical component, two digital ammeters, a power supply and some leads.

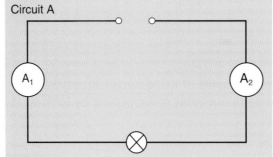

Circuit A

Set up Circuit A, as shown, and record the current at ammeters A_1 and A_2.

Now remove the lamp from the circuit and record the current at ammeters A_1 and A_2.

1 What can you learn from the readings about the current in a circuit with and without a component?

Series circuits

In the simplest circuits all the components are joined together in one loop. There are no branches or junctions. These are called series circuits.

Switch open – the switch cell and the two lamps are connected in series.	Switch closed – the circuit is complete, so both the lamps light up.

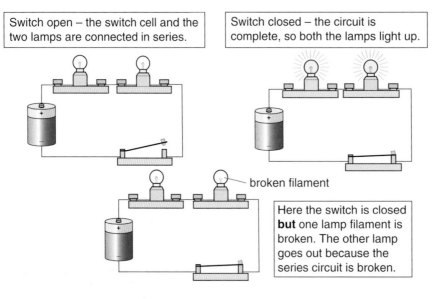

broken filament

Here the switch is closed **but** one lamp filament is broken. The other lamp goes out because the series circuit is broken.

Have you ever found that your Christmas tree lights or other fairy lights do not light up? The reason is often just one broken lamp.

The most important thing to remember about a series circuit is that every component has to be working properly or none of them will work.

Current in a series circuit

The current is the same at all places in a series circuit. This is because the current has only one pathway to flow through – there is no choice. It has to pass through all of the components and back to the power source.

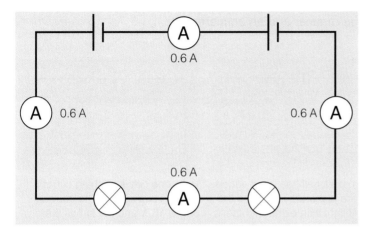

Wherever the ammeter is placed in the circuit, it gives the same reading (0.6 A). This means the current is the same everywhere in the circuit.

This result also shows that the current passes *through* the component and is *not* used up by the component.

Investigation: Measuring current in series circuits

In this experiment you will be using ammeters to measure the amount of current flowing in a series circuit.

You will need two lamps, two digital ammeters, a power supply and some leads.

Circuit B is a series combination of lamps.

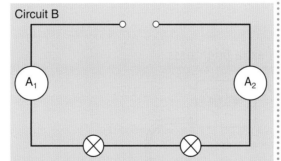

Circuit B

1 Can you predict how the current through A_1 compares with the current through A_2?
2 How do you think that the current through A_1 will compare with the current in **Circuit A** in the last investigation?

Set up this circuit and record the currents at ammeters A_1 and A_2.

3 Complete the following sentence:
In **Circuit B** with two lamps in series, the current is **larger/smaller** than in **Circuit A** with only one lamp. This shows that in a series combination it is **easier/harder** for current to flow.

Preliminary knowledge: Extra cells and components

The more cells we add into the series circuit, the greater the amount of current that will be 'pushed' around it. Any bulbs in the circuit will be brighter or an ammeter will give a higher reading. If more bulbs or other components are added to the circuit then it will be more difficult for current to flow. Bulbs will be dimmer and an ammeter will give a lower reading.

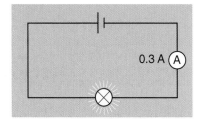

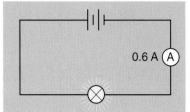

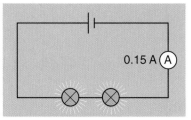

In this circuit, one cell can make a current of 0.3 A flow through one lamp.

Here an extra cell has been added. Now there is more current and the lamp will light with extra brightness.

Here one cell is pushing current through two lamps. The current is only 0.15 A and the lamps merely glow dimly.

Modelling current flow

A model of current flow may help you understand what is going on.

This model of current flow shows how a second pump in the circuit increases the flow of the ball bearings, which makes the paddle wheel turn faster. In an electrical circuit this means that:

- the voltage is greater
- the current is greater
- the lamp will light with extra brightness.

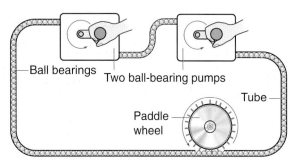

Ball bearings — Two ball-bearing pumps

Tube

Paddle wheel

Likewise the model shows that when a second paddle wheel is put in the circuit, it is harder for the pump to move the ball bearings.

The ball bearings flow more slowly, so the paddle wheels turn more slowly. In an electrical circuit this would mean that:

- the voltage is the same
- the current is less
- the lamps become dimmer.

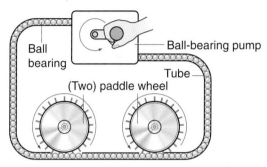

Parallel circuits

Circuits that have junctions or branches where the electrical pathway divides are called parallel circuits. In a parallel circuit, the current has more than one pathway that it could follow. Different currents can flow in parallel pathways and then join up again. This type of circuit is shown below:

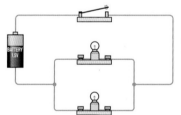

A circuit with two lamps connected in parallel.

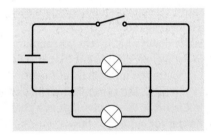

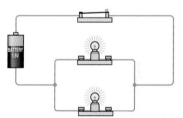

When the switch is closed, both lamps light. The switch, in this position, controls both lamps.

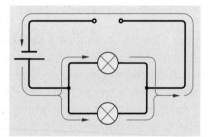

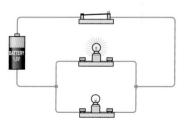

If one of the lamps blows, the other lamp stays on. There is still a complete circuit through the undamaged lamp.

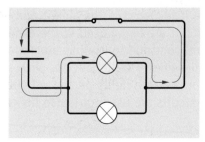

Investigation: Measuring current in parallel circuits

In this experiment you will be using ammeters to measure the amount of current flowing in a parallel circuit.

You will need two lamps, three digital ammeters, a power supply and some leads.

Set up **Circuit C** as shown.

Circuit C

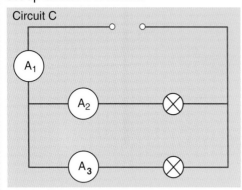

1 Can you predict how the current through A_3 will compare with the current through A_1 and A_2?

Record the currents at A_1, A_2 and A_3. Did your results confirm your prediction (at least approximately)?

2 Look at this result carefully, compare it with that of **Circuit A** in the first current investigation.
   (a) Write down what it tells you about the effect of putting components in parallel on the current that is drawn from the power supply.
   (b) Complete the following statement:
      In **Circuit C**, the current from the power supply is **larger/smaller** than in **Circuit A**. This shows that in a parallel combination it is **easier/harder** for current to flow.

3 Why is it wrong to talk of electrical components 'using up' electric current?

Remember that the current in a **series** circuit has to pass through all of the components and an ammeter will read just the same value wherever it is placed in the circuit. The current is the same everywhere in the circuit. As we have just learned, if one component isn't working, the other components will stop working, even if they are not damaged.

The current in a **parallel** circuit, however, depends on the number of choices it has. An ammeter shows a different reading depending on where it is placed in the circuit and how many of the parallel lines in the circuit are being used at the time. If one component fails, the others will continue to work as long as they are in a different one of the parallel lines. Parallel circuits with switches (see below) will allow you to turn certain lights on and off without affecting the others. Parallel circuits are used for house lights and power points.

Two models of parallel circuits

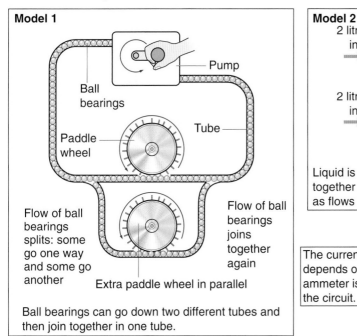

Model 1

Pump

Ball bearings

Paddle wheel

Tube

Flow of ball bearings splits: some go one way and some go another

Flow of ball bearings joins together again

Extra paddle wheel in parallel

Ball bearings can go down two different tubes and then join together in one tube.

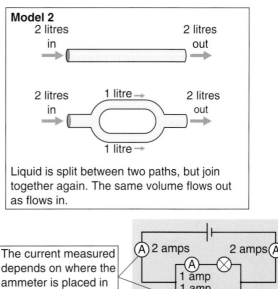

Model 2

2 litres in — 2 litres out

2 litres in — 1 litre → — 2 litres out

1 litre →

1 litre →

Liquid is split between two paths, but join together again. The same volume flows out as flows in.

The current measured depends on where the ammeter is placed in the circuit.

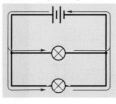

(A) 2 amps   2 amps (A)

(A) 1 amp

1 amp

(A)

Working in parallel

If you look at the diagram below, you will see that in a parallel circuit each lamp is connected directly to the power supply. The voltage (push) from the power source to the lamps is the same in each case. This means that all the lamps will shine brightly. You can connect as many lamps as you like in parallel and they will always stay the same brightness. However, when you connect more lamps in parallel, the current drawn from the battery increases. A battery will quickly run down if it has a lot of lamps connected across it in parallel.

One lamp

The current flows through the lamp and the lamp is bright.

Two lamps in parallel

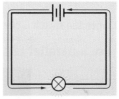

The current flows through both lamps. The lamps remain bright but twice as much current must flow from the power supply.

Switches in parallel circuits

Switches can be very useful in parallel circuits because they allow you to choose how much of a circuit the current will pass through. This illustration shows how switches can be used in this way:

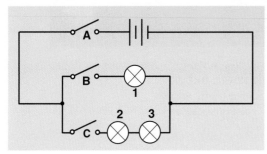

Switch **A**: Controls all bulbs
Switch **B**: Controls bulb **1**
Switch **C**: Controls bulb **2** and **3**

To light lamp **1**: **A** and **B** must be closed.

To light lamps **2** and **3**: **A** and **C** must be closed.

To light lamps **1,2** and **3**: **A,B** and **C** must be closed.

◯ Series or parallel?

When an electrician designs an electric circuit, he or she needs to decide whether a series or a parallel circuit will be best. Generally, a parallel circuit is better if the user needs to be able to control a number of components separately, but this type of circuit does take a lot of current from the power supply. A series circuit is safer because the current is smaller and is useful if you need to light several bulbs at the same time without any of them having to be particularly bright.

Using the knowledge: Series or parallel?

Fairy lights (Christmas tree lights) use a **series** circuit.

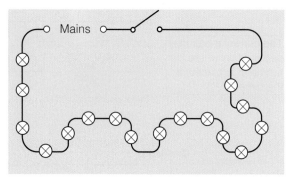

■ All the lights are lit when the switch is closed.

Household lights use a **parallel** circuit.

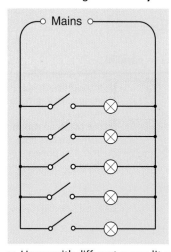

■ House with different rooms lit and unlit

Series circuit	Parallel circuit
One lamp damaged, none will light	One lamp damaged, others will still light
One switch operates all the lamps	Each lamp can be controlled by its own switch
Voltage from power supply is shared between all the lamps	Voltage across each lamp is the same as the voltage. across the power supply
Current from the power supply is low: *safer* and *cheaper to use*	Current from the power supply is high: *more dangerous* and *more expensive*

Which type of circuit would you use if you needed the lights to be on for a long time and if there was a chance that a toddler might be able to reach them?

Exercise 9.2: Series and parallel circuits

1 Match these symbols with their use. Match the letter for the symbol with the number that describes the use:

Symbol	Use
(A) ⊗	(1) Uses electric power to make a sound
(B) —(M)—	(2) Can break a circuit
(C) ⊐|	(3) Provides power for a circuit
(D) —∿°—	(4) Uses electric power to produce light
(E) ⊣⊢	(5) Uses electric power to produce movement

2 Complete this paragraph about electric circuits. Use words from this list; you may not need to use them all.

cell   buzzer   lead   current   switch
components   lamp   conductor   filament

Electricity can pass through any material that is a _____ . A complete circuit lets _____ flow all the way round it. The energy can be supplied by a _____ and can pass from one component to another through a _____ . When a circuit is made up, it may include a _____ , which can be opened to stop the flow of current. If the switch is closed, then a component such as a _____ will light or a _____ will sound.

3 Complete this table to compare series and parallel circuits:

Feature	Series circuit	Parallel circuit
Current in different places		
Number of pathways that current can take		
Effect of one damaged component		
Effect of opening a switch		

4 Look at the circuit in the diagram. A current of 2.6 A flows through ammeter C when switch 1 and switch 2 are closed:

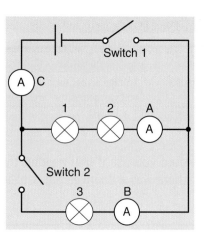

(a) What will happen to each of the lamps when switch 1 is closed with switch 2 open?

(b) If ammeter B has a reading of 1.6 A when switch 1 and switch 2 are closed, what will be the reading of ammeter A?

(c) What will be the reading on ammeter A if switch 1 is closed and switch 2 is open?

5 Six lamps were connected in a series circuit to a power supply. Six identical lamps were connected in a parallel circuit to an identical power supply.

(a) In which circuit would the lamps be brightest?

(b) Which circuit would have the highest voltage across each lamp?

(c) Which circuit would be the cheapest to use (i.e. would use the least electricity)?

Extension questions

6 Find a simple electric toy or model. Try to draw a circuit diagram for your model. Don't forget to use the correct symbols.

7 The car shown in this photograph has two headlight lamps and two rear lights connected in parallel with the car's battery.

(a) Draw a circuit diagram to show how the four lamps are connected to the battery. Include in your diagram one switch that would allow the driver to switch all the lights on or off.

(b) Use the diagram to explain why damage to one lamp will allow the other three to continue to shine.

8 An electrical contractor sells lighting systems to fairgrounds. He wants to design a system with 20 lamps: 4 red, 4 yellow, 4 green, 4 clear and 4 blue. He wants to be able to turn all 4 lamps of the same colour on or off at the same time. If a lamp of one colour blows (stops working), all the lamps of that colour could be off but the other colours should still be capable of being switched on. Design a suitable circuit for this contractor.

Problems with circuits

If a circuit doesn't work, there may be a very simple explanation:

- The circuit could be incomplete, which means the current can't flow around the circuit (e.g. a broken wire, a wire not connected to the power supply, a broken lamp filament).
- The polarity of cells is incorrect. If you are using more than one cell, they must all be the same way round.

Finding faults

A fault is something that stops an electrical circuit from working. You may have a torch that doesn't work, and this is probably due to a fault in the circuit. Some possible faults are shown in the diagram below:

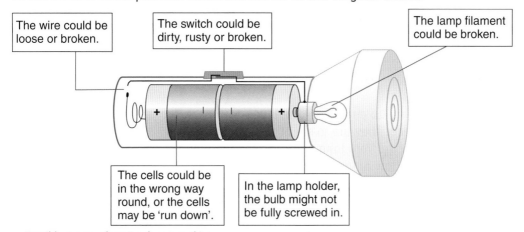

The wire could be loose or broken.

The switch could be dirty, rusty or broken.

The lamp filament could be broken.

The cells could be in the wrong way round, or the cells may be 'run down'.

In the lamp holder, the bulb might not be fully screwed in.

■ Possible reasons for a torch not working

You can find a single fault by replacing each component one at a time, until the torch starts to work again. However, this is not much use if there is more than one fault in the circuit. The second way to test for faults is to take each component and test it separately. You can do this by putting it into a circuit that you *know* is working properly.

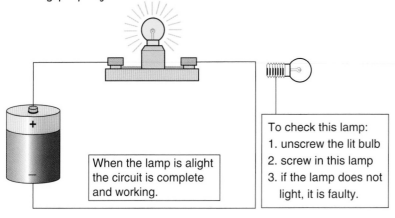

When the lamp is alight the circuit is complete and working.

To check this lamp:
1. unscrew the lit bulb
2. screw in this lamp
3. if the lamp does not light, it is faulty.

Voltage, current and resistance

In a complete circuit, the current can flow because the power supply provides a voltage to 'push' the electric charge. There are some rules to remember:

- Larger voltages cause larger currents.
- A battery or cell cannot always give the same current. The current that flows depends on what is in the circuit connected to the battery.
- Some components allow electricity to pass easily; we say that these have a **low** resistance. Other components make it hard for current to flow; we say that these have a **high resistance**.

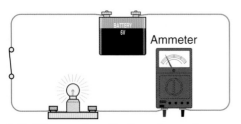 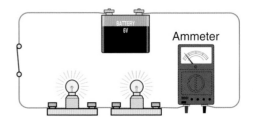

▪ Resistance reduces the flow of current

The wires used for connecting up circuits in the laboratory or in the home have a very low resistance. They are made of copper, which is a very good conductor of electricity. Very long wires, or very thin wires, make it difficult for current to flow around a circuit.

Controlling the current

Reducing the flow of current is not always a problem. When we want to control the current, we can use a resistor. The diagram below shows a resistor and how it can be useful in a circuit.

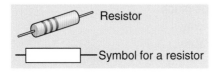 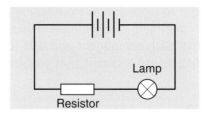

In this circuit a resistor is connected in series with the lamp. This protects the lamp, because extra resistance in the circuit means that the lamp won't blow.

You can change the flow of current through a circuit by using different resistors – high, medium and low, for example – but it is more accurate to use a **variable resistor**. A common kind of variable resistor has a very long coil of wire and a sliding contact. The sliding contact allows you to control the length of the wire that is included in the circuit and so control the amount of current that is able to flow.

> **Did you know?**
> A dimmer switch controls room lighting with a variable resistor.

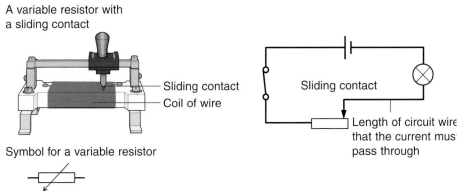

A variable resistor with a sliding contact

— Sliding contact
— Coil of wire

Symbol for a variable resistor

Sliding contact

Length of circuit wire that the current must pass through

■ Variable resistors can control current

Short circuits: Taking the easy route

Electricity takes the easiest route in a circuit. A short circuit occurs when the electric current is able to flow around the circuit without going through any components (i.e. without doing any work). This sometimes means that it is taking the **shortest** route (thus the name), but sometimes it will take a longer (but easier) route to avoid passing through a component (which is hard work!).

The diagram shows some problems due to short circuits.

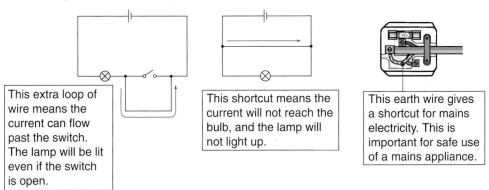

This extra loop of wire means the current can flow past the switch. The lamp will be lit even if the switch is open.

This shortcut means the current will not reach the bulb, and the lamp will not light up.

This earth wire gives a shortcut for mains electricity. This is important for safe use of a mains appliance.

You could be in danger if there is some faulty wiring in a mains appliance. The current might try to flow through you instead of through the circuit. This is why plugs have an **earth** wire. If there is some faulty wiring that causes a short circuit, the earth wire lets the current take a shortcut to the ground instead of through your body.

> If you make a circuit, be sure there are no short circuits like these. A good tip is to trace the path of the current with your finger.

1 Look at these two circuits. Which part of each circuit will the current miss out?

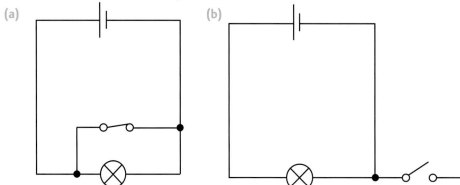

(a)   (b)

Extension questions

2 Draw a circuit diagram to show the possible faults you could find in a torch.

3 Abed and Jenny were interested in the factors that affected the resistance of a wire. They were given the following pieces of apparatus:

Battery	Switch	Ammeter
Roll of thick copper wire	Roll of thin copper wire	Roll of thin steel wire

(a) Draw a circuit that they could use in their investigation.
(b) Explain how they could carry out a fair test to see whether the thickness or length of wire is more important in affecting resistance.

Working Scientifically

10 More electrical components

You have learned that a complete electrical circuit has a power supply, a set of leads (wires) and one or more components. Components in an electrical circuit transform electrical energy into another useful form.

Each electrical component can be recognised by a symbol that is used when drawing circuit diagrams. We have already seen a number of components in electrical circuits (Chapter 9). There are many other components that are useful in everyday life. Some of these are shown in these tables.

Component and symbol	Uses	Example
Fuse	This breaks a circuit if the current becomes too great in the wire. Too much current can cause damage, or even fire.	Fuse in plug
LDR (light-dependent resistor)	These are components with a resistance that depends on light intensity. Usually the resistance is low in bright light and high in the dark. They are important in systems controlled by light intensity, such as automatic security lights and the driving lights on some cars.	Lights on a Volvo car
LED (light-emitting diode)	These are small lamps used in electronic circuits, and give a very bright light when only a small current flows. They are used as indicator lamps in many electronic devices, such as 'on' signals for games consoles. They are also used in flashing cycle lights.	Cycle light

Component and symbol	Uses	Example
Thermistor 	This has a resistance that changes according to temperature, so its resistance is usually high when cold and lower when warm. It is used in fire alarms or in frost-warning systems for greenhouses.	Fire alarm
Transistor (semiconductor diode) 	A transistor is a small, electronically controlled switch. These switches direct small currents into different circuits. Integrated circuits (ICs) contain many transistors in a single chip. These are important in computers and in the control systems for cars and motorbikes.	Motorbike

◯.Fuses

Fuses are particularly important components in electrical circuits because they play a part in the safe use of electrical appliances. There is a piece of wire inside a fuse. If the flow of current is too great, the wire becomes very hot and eventually melts. A high flow of current can be very dangerous. It could lead to electric shock or to a fire, but once the wire melts the circuit is broken and no current can flow.

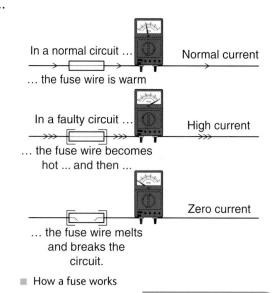

In a normal circuit …
 … the fuse wire is warm — Normal current

In a faulty circuit …
 … the fuse wire becomes hot … and then … — High current

… the fuse wire melts and breaks the circuit. — Zero current

■ How a fuse works

Exercise 10.1: Other components

1 Why is a fuse an important part of a plug that connects an appliance to the mains?

2 Sometimes a person replaces a fuse with a piece of metal foil. Why is this dangerous?

> DANGER! Too much current could make an appliance live and give an electric shock. Many house fires are started by heated wires in appliances without the correct fuse.

More about switches and control

You have learned that electric current can pass only through a complete circuit and that electric current is needed for a component of a circuit to work. In Chapter 9 you learned about how switches control electrical circuits.

Electricians can be given problems to solve. Often these problems involve providing an ideal circuit for the safe and efficient use of a machine. These circuits are likely to include switches.

A set of switches connected together are used to 'make decisions' and only allow information (electric current) through if the correct combination of switches is closed. Here are some examples of the sort of problem an electrician may have to solve:

Problem 1: An electric grinding wheel must not be operated unless the safety screen is in position.

Solution: There are two switches arranged in series. One switch is the on/off switch for the grinding wheel. The other switch is on when the safety screen is in the correct position. The motor will only run if switch A *AND* switch B are on. This arrangement is called an AND circuit, and is shown right:

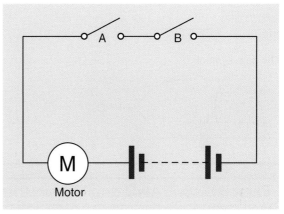

■ AND circuit: Both switch A **AND** switch B must be on before the motor will run.

Truth tables can be used to show the action of switches in circuits. A truth table shows what happens for all the possible positions of the switches. This is a truth table for an AND circuit.

Inputs		Output
Switch A	Switch B	Motor
Open	Open	Off
Open	Closed	Off
Closed	Open	Off
Closed	Closed	On

Problem 2: An alarm must go off if either the newsagent's door or the back window is opened.

Solution: To solve this problem two switches are arranged in parallel. The alarm will sound if either switch A *OR* switch B is on (closed). A circuit that makes this kind of decision is called an OR circuit.

The diagram on the right shows the operation of an OR circuit.

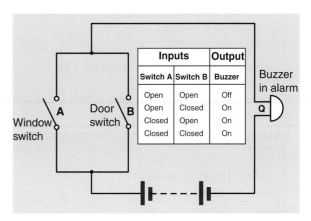

Inputs		Output
Switch A	Switch B	Buzzer
Open	Open	Off
Open	Closed	On
Closed	Open	On
Closed	Closed	On

■ OR circuit: If either switch A **OR** switch B is on the alarm will sound.

Go further

AND and OR circuits can either allow current to pass (1) or not (0). These circuits are often called **gates**, for they open and close like gates in a field. We refer to these as an **AND gate** and an **OR gate**. Both AND and OR gates have symbols for use when drawing circuit diagrams. These are shown below.

AND gate symbol

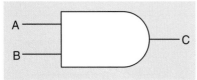

OR gate symbol

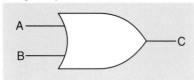

■ Electronic equipment uses integrated circuits (chips) that have many logic gates packed together into one tiny component.

Exercise 10.2: AND and OR circuits

1 Choose the **best** answer:
   An AND circuit will allow current to flow if:
   (a) either switch is closed.
   (b) the current flowing through two switches can be added together.
   (c) both of the switches are closed.
   (d) the current is increased.

2 Choose the **best** answer:
   An OR gate will allow current to flow if:
   (a) either switch is closed.
   (b) the current flowing through two switches can be added together.
   (c) both of the switches are closed.
   (d) the current is increased.

3 The diagram shows a circuit containing a buzzer, a lamp and three switches.
   Complete the table below to show what happens to the lamp and the buzzer in each case.

Switch 1	Switch 2	Switch 3	Buzzer	Lamp
Closed	Closed	Closed		
Closed	Open	Closed		
Closed	Closed	Open		
Open	Closed	Closed		
Open	Open	Closed		

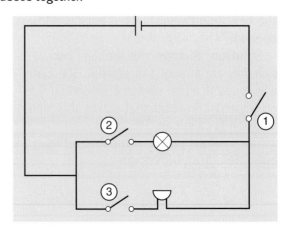

138

11 Magnets and magnetic fields

We can sometimes find rocks in the ground that attract objects made from iron or steel. This pulling force is called magnetism. These naturally occurring magnetic rocks are called **lodestones** and exert a pulling force on the iron in the object.

Scientists can make magnets that work just like these magnetic rocks. These magnets are more useful than magnetic rocks because they can be made much stronger and be fashioned into many different shapes and sizes. These modern magnets can be used for many different jobs, e.g. fridge magnets, magnetised strips for closing doors and compasses.

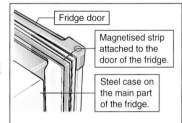

Fridge door

Magnetised strip attached to the door of the fridge.

Steel case on the main part of the fridge.

A compass uses a magnet to point to the NORTH and SOUTH.

NORTH (the direction NORTH depends on the magnetic rocks in the Earth).

This end of the magnet points NORTH. We call it the **NORTH-SEEKING POLE** of the magnet.

The case of the magnet **must** be made of a non-magnetic material (e.g. brass).

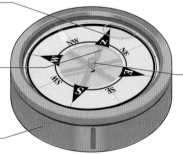

Look at Chemistry, Chapter 5, to see how magnets are used in separating mixtures that include iron.

The needle in a compass is a small magnet. The magnet is mounted on a pivot so that it can swing freely in any direction.

Magnetic forces

Each magnet has two ends, called poles. The names of these poles come from the direction in which a moving magnet points when it is affected by the magnetic rocks in the Earth.

Preliminary knowledge: Forces of attraction

The poles of magnets exert forces on one another. These are shown in the diagram on the next page.

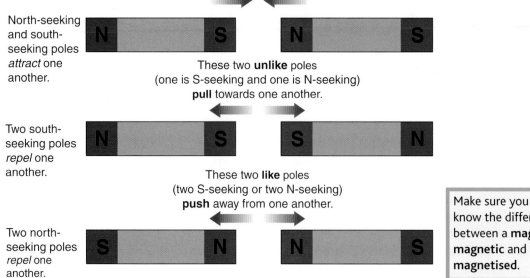

North-seeking and south-seeking poles *attract* one another.

These two **unlike** poles
(one is S-seeking and one is N-seeking)
pull towards one another.

Two south-seeking poles *repel* one another.

These two **like** poles
(two S-seeking or two N-seeking)
push away from one another.

Two north-seeking poles *repel* one another.

> Make sure you know the difference between a **magnet**, **magnetic** and **magnetised**.

An object can be magnetic but *not* be a magnet. For example, a piece of iron is magnetic (it is attracted to a magnet) but does not act like a magnet itself. One piece of iron does not attract or repel another piece of iron.

The only way to test if a material or object is a magnet is to test for repulsion by a known magnet.

Finding the poles of a magnet

Each magnet has a north-seeking and a south-seeking pole. You can find which pole is which by hanging the magnet up or floating it in liquid and seeing whether it points north or south. An easier way to do this is to use a compass.

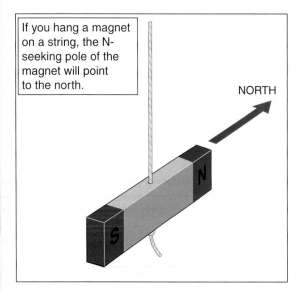

If you hang a magnet on a string, the N-seeking pole of the magnet will point to the north.

NORTH

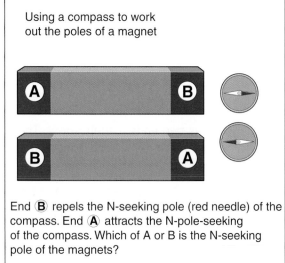

Using a compass to work out the poles of a magnet

End **B** repels the N-seeking pole (red needle) of the compass. End **A** attracts the N-pole-seeking of the compass. Which of A or B is the N-seeking pole of the magnets?

140

A compass works in this way because the compass needle is itself a magnet. The needle points north–south because the Earth is also a magnet (a giant one!). The compass needle lines up with the Earth's **magnetic field** (see below). If we know that the north-seeking pole of the compass needle always points towards the Earth's North Pole, we can work out the direction in which we are travelling. Hill walkers and explorers can use a compass and a map to find out where they are and to work out in which direction to walk to find a particular place and not get lost.

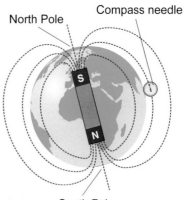

The Earth is a giant magnet. Note that the compass would be held parallel to the Earth's surface.

Magnetic materials can cause problems

Most substances are not magnetic. Iron is the most important magnetic element, but nickel and cobalt are also magnetic. Alloys – such as steel – that contain any of these elements are magnetic too. If you are trying to use a compass to find your way, it is important to make sure that there is no magnetic material nearby. These elements are found in rocks in the Earth's crust, and some electrical equipment is magnetic. In some parts of Scotland the rocks are so magnetic that a compass would just make you walk in circles!

A compass needle can be attracted to magnetic rocks instead of being lined up with the Earth's magnetic field

◯ Magnetic fields

If you bring a metal object towards a magnet, you will feel the pull of the magnet before the object and the magnet actually touch one another. This means that magnetism must be reaching out into the air around the magnet. Because magnetism is able to push or pull another object, we know that **magnetism is a force**.

We can use a compass needle or iron filings to show the pattern of this magnetic force around a magnet:

1 Place a magnet on some card.
2 Sprinkle iron filings on the card.
3 Each filing then becomes magnetised and lines up with the magnetic field of the magnet.
4 The pattern of the filings shows us the **shape** of the magnetic field (see diagram on the next page).

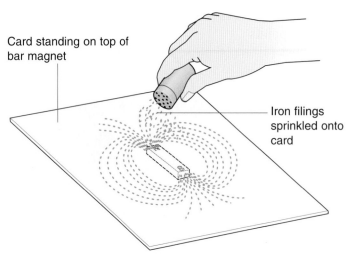

Card standing on top of bar magnet

Iron filings sprinkled onto card

The field is actually in three dimensions around the magnet.

Look at these patterns and compare them with the Earth's magnetic field shown earlier in this chapter.

■ The magnetic field of a magnet

Here's another way to see the magnetic field:

- Use a small compass (a plotting compass) to trace the lines of the magnetic field.
- The compass needle can rotate and so will show the **direction** of the magnetic field as well as its shape.

When you draw a magnetic field, the lines showing the direction of the field should have arrows pointing away from the north-seeking pole.

This pattern of magnetic force is called a magnetic field. Any object inside the magnetic field will be affected by the magnetic force. The magnetic field is strongest where the lines of magnetic force are closest together and weakest where the lines are far apart.

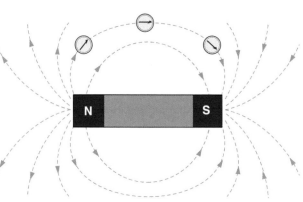

Exercise 11.1: Magnets

1 Fill in the gaps to complete these sentences using words from the following list:

poles   iron   repel   north   attract

(a) A magnet can be hung up so that it can move easily. If this happens, one end will point _____ and the other end will point south. The two different ends of a magnet are called the _____ . Magnets exert forces on materials that contain _____ .

(b) Like poles of magnets _____ one another, but unlike poles _____ .

2 Make a copy of this table. Complete the table to show you understand the forces between magnets.

Pole of first magnet	Pole of second magnet	Do they attract or repel?	Is this a push or a pull?
N	S		
N	N		
S	S		

3 (a) Draw a diagram to explain how a compass works.

(b) Explain how magnetic objects can make a compass unreliable.

Working Scientifically

Electricity and magnetism

As you have learned, magnetism is a force. A magnet has a magnetic field that exists in three dimensions all around it.

A piece of steel that has been magnetised so that it keeps its magnetic properties is called a **permanent magnet**.

Scientists in the early nineteenth century discovered that an electric current (see Chapter 9) also exerts a magnetic force. This means that we can use electricity to make magnets, called electromagnets. Electromagnets can be turned on and off. Much of our modern technology depends on this.

Linking electricity and magnetism

The circuit shown below shows that there is a magnetic field around a wire that is carrying an electric current. This link between electric current and magnetism is called **electromagnetism**.

The magnetic field around an ordinary electric wire is not very strong, but its shape can be shown using plotting compasses and the apparatus shown below:

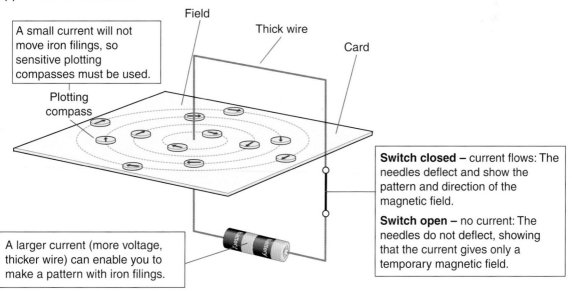

A small current will not move iron filings, so sensitive plotting compasses must be used.

A larger current (more voltage, thicker wire) can enable you to make a pattern with iron filings.

Switch closed – current flows: The needles deflect and show the pattern and direction of the magnetic field.

Switch open – no current: The needles do not deflect, showing that the current gives only a temporary magnetic field.

■ A magnetic field around a wire

Hans Christian Oersted

Hans Christian Oersted (1777–1851) was a Danish physicist and chemist. At the start of the nineteenth century he spent some time travelling across Europe and met German scientist Johann Wilhelm Ritter, who believed there was a connection between electricity and magnetism. It was after this meeting that Oersted's interest in magnetism began. In 1806 he became a professor at the University of Copenhagen.

In 1820 Oersted noticed that a compass needle moved from magnetic north when an electric current was switched on and off in a circuit placed close to the compass. This confirmed, for the first time, a direct relationship between electricity and magnetism.

Oersted's experiments: The Danish scientist Oersted showed the effect of an electric current on a compass needle.

1. Switch open: There is no current flow. See how the compass needle lines up with the Earth's field.

2. Switch closed: The current flows. The compass needle is deflected and lines up with the magnetic field around the wire.

3. Switch closed but current reversed: The compass needle is deflected in the opposite direction because the lines of force in the magnetic field are now running in the opposite direction.

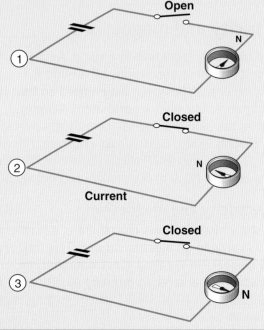

Investigation: The strength of an electromagnetic field

The aim of this investigation is to study the strength of an electromagnetic field.

A current flowing through a coiled wire acts like a magnet.

 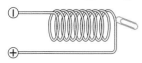 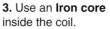

1. Use a **bigger** current.	**2.** Put more **turns** of wire on the coil.	**3.** Use an **Iron core** inside the coil.
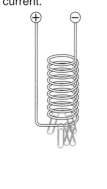	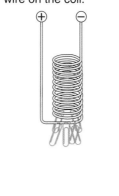	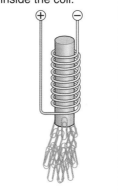

To make this a fair test, keep:
- the number of coils and
- the current constant.

1 Can you think of any other factor to keep constant?

You can then check if the core material matters.

Iron core	Steel core	Glass core
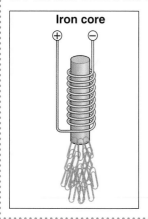	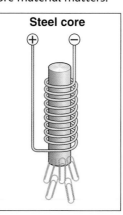	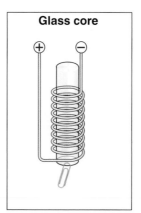

Electromagnets

A coiled wire (called a solenoid) gives a stronger field than the straight wire shown above. The field becomes even stronger if the wire is coiled around a rod of iron. The rod of iron is called the core, and the coil and core together make up an electromagnet. The field pattern around an **electromagnet** is the same as that around a bar magnet, as shown:

Making the field stronger

It is very useful to have a magnet that can be switched on and off. The pulling force of the magnet can be used to lift a magnetic object. The current can then be switched off and the magnetic material can be dropped. An electromagnet like this can be used for separating magnetic materials from non-magnetic materials, for example in a scrapyard or in a recycling centre.

As well as just switching an electromagnet on or off, it is also possible to control the strength of the magnetic field. There are three ways that this can be done:

- by increasing the electric current
- by increasing the number of coils in the solenoid
- by changing the material in the core.

The pattern and the direction of the magnetic field around an electromagnet are the same as the field around a bar magnet.

Switch

Cell

1.5V BATTERY

Coil

Core (iron)

■ The magnetic field around an electromagnet

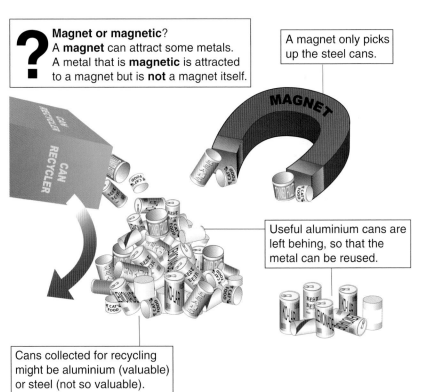

? **Magnet or magnetic?**
A **magnet** can attract some metals. A metal that is **magnetic** is attracted to a magnet but is **not** a magnet itself.

A magnet only picks up the steel cans.

Useful aluminium cans are left behing, so that the metal can be reused.

Cans collected for recycling might be aluminium (valuable) or steel (not so valuable).

◯ More uses for electromagnets

So we now know that electromagnets can be switched on and off.
This makes them very useful in many ways:

Magnets and medicine

Electromagnets are used:

- to remove metal splinters from wounds

- to look inside the body, using Magnetic Resonance Imaging (MRI) [see photograph].

An electric bell

- Switch (1) is closed, usually by pushing a button.

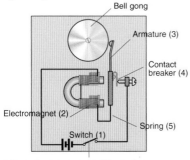

- The electromagnet (2) produces a pulling force.
- The armature (3) is pulled towards (2), so the gong strikes the bell.
- The contact breaker (4) breaks the circuit, so the pulling force stops.
- The spring (5) pushes the armature back, the circuit is complete again and the whole cycle is repeated... RRRIIIIIINNNGGG!

ELECTRO-MAGNETS ARE USEFUL

A **relay** is an electrically-controlled switch.
The circuit symbol for a relay is:

relay
(normally open)

This uses a **small** current to turn on another circuit. The second circuit may carry a **large** current, needed to turn a powerful motor.

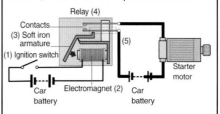

Relay (4)

Contacts
(3) Soft iron
armature
(1) Ignition switch

(5)

Starter
motor

Car
battery   Electromagnet (2)   Car
battery

- The ignition switch (1) is closed and a small (safe!) current flows to the electromagnet (2).

- The armature (3) is pulled across to the electromagnet.

- A pivot in (3) means the contacts (4) are pushed together so that the second circuit (5) is completed.

- A large current flows in (5) to turn the starter motor (see Exercise 11.2 question 4 for circuit diagram)'

A **reed switch** is a small relay used in electronic circuits.
The circuit symbol for a reed switch is:

reed switch

The reed switch has thin metal contacts inside a glass tube.

no magnet:
switch open

A magnet can bring the contacts together in a normally-open (NO) switch.

magnet nearby:
switch closed

In a normally-closed (NC) switch the magnet keeps the contacts apart. **Removing** the magnet makes the contacts move together. An NC reed switch can be used in a simple burglar alarm.

electromagnet on:
switch closed

bell

NC reed
switch

Magnetic trains

Monorail train systems, like those at Disneyworld, use electromagnets to 'float' about 15 mm above the track. This gives a very smooth ride, and saves wear on the wheels and track.

Exercise 11.2: Electromagnetism

1 What is the main reason for using a relay to switch on an electric motor?
   (a) It is cheap to buy.
   (b) It only uses a small current to start a motor.
   (c) It is very easy to connect into a circuit.
   (d) It can pass a current from a battery into a motor

2 How would the pulling force of an electromagnet be affected by:
   (a) Changing the iron core for a copper core?
   (b) Increasing the current through the coils?
   (c) Using a coil with fewer turns?
   (d) Changing the iron core for a steel core?

3 Look at the diagram of the relay in the section 'More uses for electromagnets'.
   (a) Copy out the diagram with the switch in the closed position. Use a red pencil or pen to trace the flow of current through this circuit.
   (b) Show in your diagram where the largest current would be measured.

4 Look at the circuit diagram below. Redraw it to show what happens when the driver of a car closes the ignition switch by using a key.

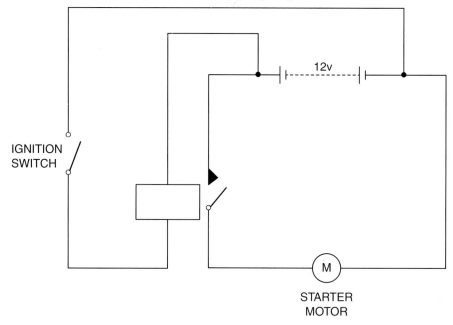

IGNITION
SWITCH

12v

M

STARTER
MOTOR

Extension question

5 Describe how you would investigate how the number of coils in an electromagnet affects the strength of the magnetic field. In your answer you should include:
   (a) diagrams of the apparatus set up for use
   (b) any steps taken to make sure that this is a fair test
   (c) the results you might expect to get.

12 Space physics

Our Solar System

We live on the Earth but we can see the Sun and the Moon quite clearly. We can see the Sun because it is the source of all our light in the Solar System – we call the Sun a **luminous source**. Other stars are also light sources.

We can see the Moon because it's quite close to us and reflects light from the Sun.

We can also see the other planets (some with the aid of telescopes) even though they are not light sources. This is because they too reflect light from the Sun.

The Sun is an enormous, very hot ball of glowing gas called a star. It produces all the thermal energy and light necessary for life on Earth. The Earth is much smaller and cooler, and is one of the planets that move around the Sun. The Sun and the planets that move around it make up most of our Solar System.

There are also moons, which are large bodies or satellites that orbit some of the planets (this includes our Moon) and thousands of large lumps of rock called asteroids in a belt between the fourth and fifth planets.

The Sun, Moon, Earth and other planets are approximately spherical.

> Look back at Chapter 8 to remind yourself about light, light sources and reflection.

> Remember: Water boils at 100 °C and freezes at 0 °C.
>
> Earth is the only planet in our Solar System that has liquid water. All life depends on the presence of water so the only planet where living things are known to exist is Earth.
>
> Scientists sending probes to other planets look for evidence for the presence of liquid water, either now or in the past.

Go further

■ Features of the planets

Planet	Average distance from Sun, in million km	Diameter, in km	Orbit time, in days	Average temperature, in °C	Number of moons
Neptune	4495	49 528	59 800	−200	14
Uranus	2873	51 118	30 589	−195	27
Saturn	1434	120 536	10 747	−140	62
Jupiter	779	142 987	4331	−110	67
ASTEROID BELT					
Mars	228	6792	687	−65	2
Earth	150	12 756	365.2	15	1
Venus	108	12 104	224.7	464	0
Mercury	58	4879	88	167	0

Source: nssdc.gsfc.nasa.gov/planetary/factsheet

Pluto, discovered in 1930, was originally classified as the ninth planet from the Sun. In 2006 the International Astronomical Union (IAU) redefined the term 'planet' and Pluto failed to meet one of the conditions of the redefinition. These conditions were that the celestial body had to be round, orbit the Sun and have a clear pathway within its orbit, and Pluto seemed to have many other small celestial bodies inside its orbit.

Pluto was given the new classification as a 'dwarf planet'. Other celestial bodies have been granted dwarf planet status on the basis of the reclassification. This means that we now consider the Solar System to be made up of eight planets and a number of dwarf planets.

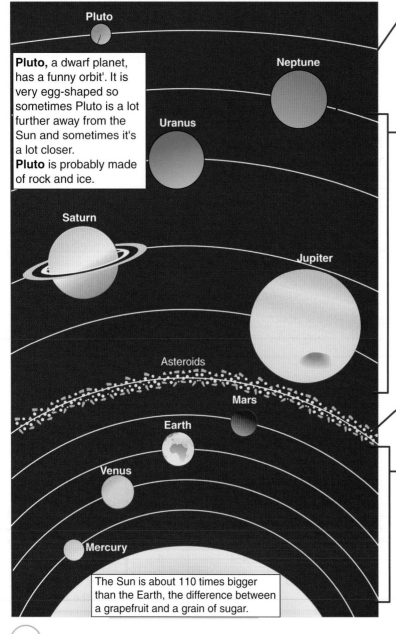

Pluto

Pluto, a dwarf planet, has a funny orbit'. It is very egg-shaped so sometimes Pluto is a lot further away from the Sun and sometimes it's a lot closer.
Pluto is probably made of rock and ice.

Neptune

Uranus

Saturn

Jupiter

Asteroids

Mars

Earth

Venus

Mercury

The Sun is about 110 times bigger than the Earth, the difference between a grapefruit and a grain of sugar.

The path taken by each planet around the Sun is called the **orbit.** The planets keep in their orbits by the force of **gravity.**

The outer planets: These are large, low density, with deep atmospheres and no solid surface. Saturn's rings are millions of bits of rock and ice in orbit.

Remembering names can be difficult! Make up a silly story to help you remember the order of the eight planets and the dwarf planet Pluto.

My Very Eccentric Mother Just Shot Uncle Norman's Pig

The asteroids are thousands of minor planets. The largest is only 1000 km across.

The inner planets are small and dense, and are mainly made of rock and iron.

The Solar System is too big for sizes and distances to be shown on some diagrams. In this diagram, sizes are approximately to scale but distances from the Sun are not.

Scientists are always willing to review their conclusions when new evidence is obtained. In October 2014, astronomers at Johns Hopkins University presented evidence that Pluto might deserve to be considered a planet again!

◯ Preliminary knowledge: Day and night

Before we move on, it is worth just checking that you have remembered how we get night and day and how shadows are formed. Both of these can be explained by the way in which the Earth moves in relation to the Sun.

The way in which the Earth moves in space gives us day and night. The reasons for this are as follows:

- The Earth slowly spins around the axis of the Earth (the line running from the North Pole to the South Pole). The Earth's axis is tilted at an angle.
- It takes one **day** (24 hours) for the Earth to go through one complete turn.
- Light from the Sun shines on the Earth and lights up the half of the earth facing it. It is **daytime** on this side.
- The side of the Earth away from the Sun is in darkness. It is **night-time** on this side.
- The continual transition from day to night and back to day is therefore caused by the rotation of the Earth around this axis so that any location on Earth moves from the lit side of the Earth into the dark side and then on into the lit side again.
- As well as giving **night** and **day**, the following movements of the Earth are also important – they affect seasons in different parts of the Earth (see later in this chapter).
- The Earth is always travelling around the Sun in an elliptical path called an orbit.
- It takes 365¼ days (one year) for the Earth to go through one complete orbit.

> It is important to note that the boundary between the lit and dark sides of the Earth is NOT tilted with the axis but is vertical. This results in the areas around the poles having parts of the year where they are in permanent darkness and parts when they are in permanent daylight.

Did you know?

Stars are still there in the day! Stars can be seen at night as the light they emit can be seen in the dark sky. During the day the stars are still there, but it is too bright (because of our star, the Sun) to see them!

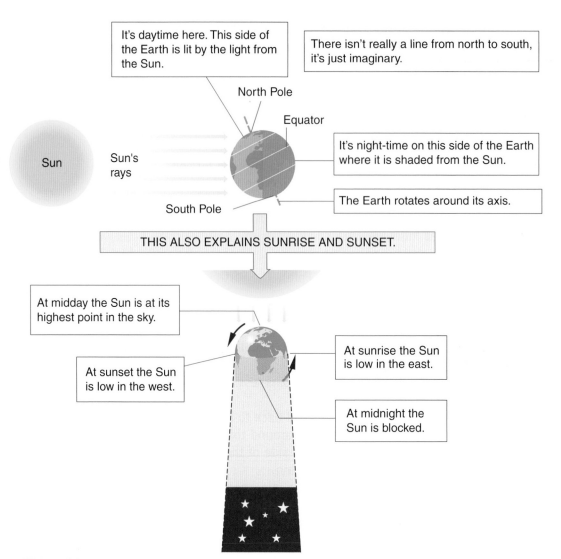

It's daytime here. This side of the Earth is lit by the light from the Sun.

There isn't really a line from north to south, it's just imaginary.

North Pole

Equator

Sun

Sun's rays

It's night-time on this side of the Earth where it is shaded from the Sun.

The Earth rotates around its axis.

South Pole

THIS ALSO EXPLAINS SUNRISE AND SUNSET.

At midday the Sun is at its highest point in the sky.

At sunrise the Sun is low in the east.

At sunset the Sun is low in the west.

At midnight the Sun is blocked.

■ Night and day

Preliminary knowledge: Sun and shadow

The Sun always stays in the same place, which is at the centre of our Solar System. The Sun *appears* to move across the sky as the day goes on because the Earth is moving. Any objects in the way of the sunlight cast a **shadow** (see Chapter 8 to remind yourself about shadows). The size and direction of the shadow depends on where the Sun is when it shines on an object.

- Shadows are short at midday because the Sun is directly overhead.
- Shadows are **long** in the morning and the evening because the Sun is low in the sky.
- The shadows are always on the opposite side of the object from the Sun.

Remember, the Sun doesn't move: the Earth does.

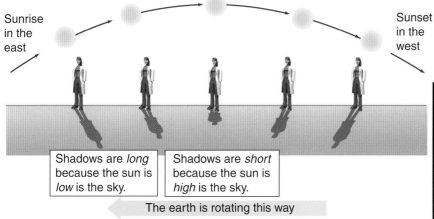

Sunrise in the east

Sunset in the west

Shadows are *long* because the sun is *low* is the sky.

Shadows are *short* because the sun is *high* is the sky.

The earth is rotating this way

Sundials use these two rules to let us tell the time. We can make a scale that the shadow can fall on. As the shadow moves, it travels across the time scale and so tells us what time of day it is.

Exercise 12.1: The Sun and the Earth

1 Complete the paragraph using words from this list:

Moon   Sun   reflected   Solar System   planet   star

The Earth is a _____ that moves around the _____ . The Sun is at the centre of the _____ and is a very hot ball of glowing gas called a _____ . The _____ travels around the Earth and we can see it because of light _____ from the Sun.

2 Use a diagram to explain why it is midday in the UK at the same time that it is midnight in Australia.

Working Scientifically

3 Why do stars only come out at night?

Extension questions

4 Scientists are very interested in the possibility of life on other planets. Give two reasons why you think that it is very unlikely that we will find organisms similar to those on Earth on any other planet.

5 What shape is the Sun? How do we know?

The year and the seasons

You have learned that the Sun is at the centre of the Solar System and that the Earth is one of the planets that move around the Sun. The Earth rotates around a line called its axis.

What is a year?

The Earth moves around the Sun in an **orbit**. The Earth is kept in this orbit by the pull of the Sun's gravity (more on gravity later in this chapter). One **year** (actually 365¼ days) is the time taken for the Earth to complete one orbit.

This would be the axis if the Earth were upright.

The spinning of the Earth.

This is the actual axis of the Earth. The tilt means that Britain has more hours of light than dark.

Sun

As you have seen, the Earth rotates around its axis to give day and night. The axis of the Earth is not exactly upright; it actually leans to one side, so that the North Pole and the South Pole don't get exactly the same amount of sunlight.

During the course of a year the North Pole is sometimes closer to the Sun and sometimes further away from the Sun. When the Earth is rotating with the North Pole nearer the Sun, it is summer in the UK (northern hemisphere) and winter at the opposite end of the Earth, for example in Australia (southern hemisphere). It is winter in the UK when the Earth is rotating with the North Pole *away from* the Sun.

The tilting of the Earth gives us the **seasons**.

> At the **equator** (equal distance between the North and South Poles) there is very little difference between summer and winter, so the changes of seasons are not as obvious as they are at the two **poles**.

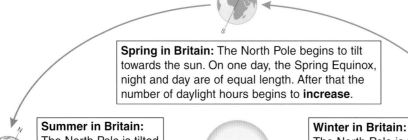

Spring in Britain: The North Pole begins to tilt towards the sun. On one day, the Spring Equinox, night and day are of equal length. After that the number of daylight hours begins to **increase**.

Summer in Britain: The North Pole is tilted towards the sun and the day is longer than the night.

SUN

Winter in Britain: The North Pole is tilted away from the sun. The night is longer than the day.

Autumn in Britain: The North Pole begins to tilt away from the Sun. On one day, the Autumn Equinox, night and day are of equal length. After that the number of daylight hours begins to **decrease**.

Space physics

The height of the Sun varies from season to season

The Sun is highest in the sky at midday (12 noon) on any given day. The Sun appears in the UK to be at its greatest height in the sky when the North Pole is tilted towards the Sun, i.e. in the summer.

Remember that the height of the Sun affects the length of shadows. The Sun is lowest during the winter, so the shadows on sunny days in winter are longer than those on sunny days in summer.

When the Sun is lower in the sky, it does not heat up the surface of the Earth as well as it does when it is high in the sky. Winter is colder because:

- the Sun is lower in the sky, so its energy does not fall so directly onto the Earth's surface
- the Sun is not shining on the Earth so long, as the days are shorter.

> Don't forget that the Earth is spinning around its North–South axis, as well as orbiting the Sun.

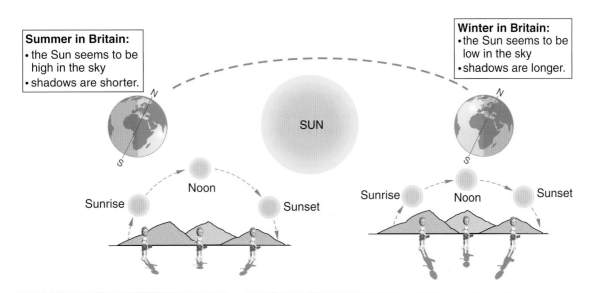

Summer in Britain:
- the Sun seems to be high in the sky
- shadows are shorter.

Winter in Britain:
- the Sun seems to be low in the sky
- shadows are longer.

What about the Moon?

Preliminary knowledge: A lunar month

The Moon is the natural satellite of the Earth. It orbits the Earth just as the Earth and the other planets orbit the Sun. It takes about 28 days for the Moon to complete one orbit of the Earth. This length of time is called a lunar month (the word 'lunar' means 'to do with the Moon').

More about the Moon

The Moon is kept in this orbit by the pull of the Earth's gravity (more on gravity later in this chapter).

The Moon is our nearest neighbour in the Solar System and is close enough to have been visited by humans. It has been studied enough to enable us produce a Moon map!

The Moon rotates once during one complete orbit of the Earth, so the same side always faces the Earth.

The **far side** of the Moon (also known as the **dark side**, when there is a full Moon) can only be seen from space.

The Moon is not **luminous,** which means it does not give out its own light but it does reflect light from the Sun.

> **Did you know?**
>
> Gravity on the Moon is only a sixth ($\frac{1}{6}$) of that on Earth. A human could pole-vault 30 metres on the Moon!

> **Did you know?**
>
> Moon days and nights last for 14 Earth days!
>
> Moon day: temperature = +123 °C
>
> Moon night: temperature = −233 °C

> The Moon has no atmosphere to support life – astronauts need a space suit with oxygen cylinders.

■ Lunar surface, the Hadley-Apennine region of the Moon. Photographed during the Apollo 15 mission of 1971

The Moon and eclipses

Lunar eclipse

A **lunar** eclipse or eclipse of the Moon happens when **the Earth comes between the Moon and the Sun**. As a lunar eclipse takes place, we can usually see the shadow of the Earth slowly moving across the face of the Moon.

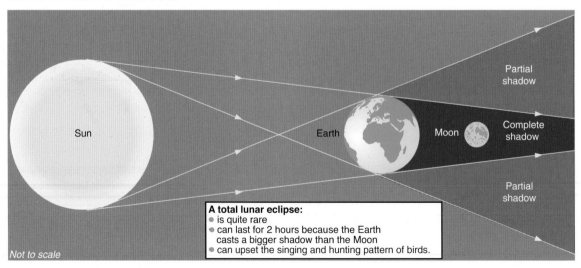

Sun

Earth

Moon

Partial shadow

Complete shadow

Partial shadow

A total lunar eclipse:
- is quite rare
- can last for 2 hours because the Earth casts a bigger shadow than the Moon
- can upset the singing and hunting pattern of birds.

Not to scale

Solar eclipse

A **solar eclipse**, otherwise known as an eclipse of the Sun, happens when **the Moon comes between the Earth and the Sun**. Light from the Sun is hidden from us on Earth and the Moon looks like a black disc surrounded by a bright ring (the corona) of the Sun.

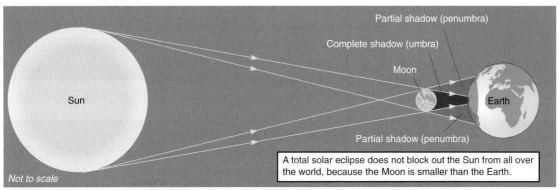

Partial shadow (penumbra)
Complete shadow (umbra)
Moon
Sun
Earth
Partial shadow (penumbra)

A total solar eclipse does not block out the Sun from all over the world, because the Moon is smaller than the Earth.

Not to scale

The Moon starts to cover the Sun.

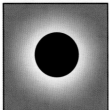

The start of totality where the Moon first covers the Sun.

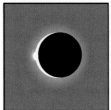

The end of totality where the Moon stops covering the Sun.

The eclipse finishes.

You must **never** look directly at the Sun! This could damage the retina and blind you, so special filters are needed to view an eclipse.

Exercise 12.2: Sun, Earth and Moon

1 How long does it take for:
   (a) the Earth to orbit the Sun?
   (b) the Moon to orbit the Earth?
   (c) the Earth to turn once on its axis?

2 Give two reasons why it is colder in winter than in summer.

3 Copy this diagram (not drawn to scale):
   (a) Shade in the part of the Earth that is in shadow.
   (b) Is it summer or winter in Britain?
   (c) Is it daytime or night-time in Britain?

4 How does a solar eclipse give us evidence that light travels in straight lines?

5 Draw a diagram showing how a lunar eclipse happens.

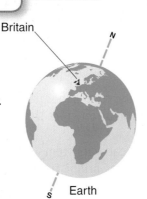

Britain
N
Sun
S   Earth

Extension questions

Working Scientifically

6 Find out what is meant by 'midnight Sun'. Use a diagram to explain how it can happen.

7 How many times does the Moon orbit the Earth while the Earth completes one orbit of the Sun? Give a reason for your answer.

The Sun and other stars

The Sun is at the centre of the Solar System. We currently know of eight planets and a number of other bodies, including dwarf planets, which orbit at great distances around the Sun.

The **Universe** contains everything that exists. The Solar System is just one part of the Universe; it is part of a **galaxy** called the **Milky Way**.

■ Milky Way galaxy seen in the night sky above a desert, California, USA

The Universe

Earth, which is part of ...

... the *Solar System*, which is part of ...

... the *Milky Way*, which is one of many galaxies in the universe.

The Universe contains many galaxies and each galaxy contains millions of **stars** together with clouds of dust and gas. The stars can be very different from one another:

- Their **size** can vary, from supergiants that are very much bigger than the Sun, to neutron stars that are only the same size as the Earth.
- Their **brightness** can vary from 100 000 times brighter than the Sun to 100 000 times less bright than the Sun.
- The **distances** between them can vary, but in every case the distance is very large indeed.

Remember that stars can be seen because they are **luminous** (i.e. they give out their own light). Size, brightness and distance from the Earth all affect how easily we can see a star. This is unlike planets and moons that are only seen because they **reflect** light from the Sun.

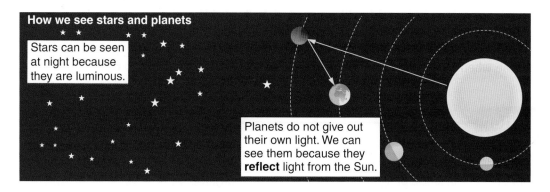

How we see stars and planets

Stars can be seen at night because they are luminous.

Planets do not give out their own light. We can see them because they **reflect** light from the Sun.

Stars are light years from Earth

Because the Universe is so large and the stars are so far away, it is not easy to measure distances in normal units such as kilometres. It is easier to use a unit called a light year. A light year is the distance travelled by light in one year. Light moves very quickly and in one year it covers 9 461 000 000 000 km.

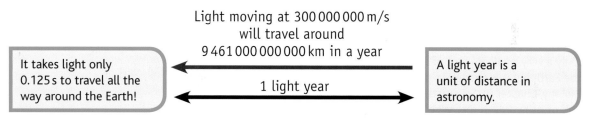

Light moving at 300 000 000 m/s will travel around 9 461 000 000 000 km in a year

It takes light only 0.125 s to travel all the way around the Earth!

A light year is a unit of distance in astronomy.

1 light year

The closest star to the Earth, other than the Sun, is 4.2 light years away and astronomers have discovered some stars that are 10 000 000 light years away. These distances are very much greater than the distances between the planets in the Solar System.

The stars in the Milky Way form patterns, called **constellations**. People have studied these constellations for thousands of years and have given them names according to their appearance from the Earth.

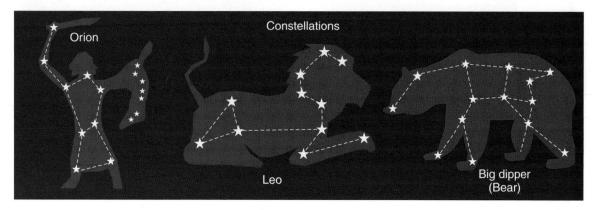

Constellations

Orion

Leo

Big dipper (Bear)

The nearest large galaxy to the Milky Way is called **Andromeda** and is 2 million light years away. When we see light from Andromeda we are actually looking at something that happened 2 million years ago, around the time when the first ape-like humans were appearing on the Earth.

Go further

The Sun is a star

Stars appear to us as tiny pinpricks of light because they are so far away. The exception is the Sun. The Sun looks very large to us because:

- it is more than a thousand times bigger than the Earth
- it is very close – only 149 million kilometres away!

The Sun was formed from gas and dust around 5 billion years ago. The gases became squashed together and hydrogen atoms combined to form helium atoms. This is a **nuclear fusion** reaction, and releases enormous amounts of thermal and light energy. Scientists think that the temperature at the centre of the Sun is as high as 14 000 000 °C, with the surface being much cooler at only 6000 °C!

Only a very small amount of the energy released from the Sun ever reaches the Earth but it is enough to provide the energy for all of our food chains (see Biology, Chapter 9). Scientists believe that the Sun has already used up about half of its hydrogen fuel. When the hydrogen runs out, the Sun will first collapse, then swell to form a huge **red giant**. The red giant will swallow up and burn Mercury, Venus and the Earth, then it will collapse again to end up as a tiny **white dwarf** star.

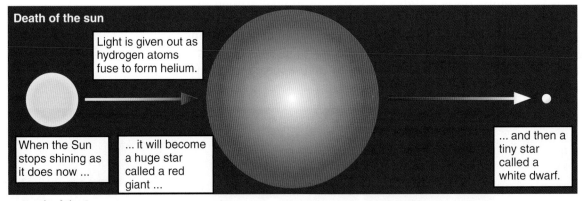

Death of the sun

Light is given out as hydrogen atoms fuse to form helium.

When the Sun stops shining as it does now ...

... it will become a huge star called a red giant ...

... and then a tiny star called a white dwarf.

■ Death of the Sun

1 Choose words from this list to fill in the gaps in the following paragraphs. You may not need to use all the words.

luminous	**Sun**	**star**	**light years**
reflection	**constellations**	**Universe**	**kilometres**

(a) We can see stars because they are _____ . The Moon and some planets are visible because of the _____ of light from the _____ . Many stars seem to be arranged in patterns called _____ .

(b) Distances in space are so great that we need to measure them in _____ . All the planets, stars, gases and dust together make up the _____ .

2 Light travels at 300 000 km per second. The Sun is 149 million kilometres from the Earth. How long does light take to reach the Earth from the Sun?

Extension question

3 Why are large telescopes for observing stars usually built on hills well away from large cities?

| Working Scientifically

4 Using the internet, write a short paragraph explaining what major reclassification was agreed by the IAU on 24 August 2006.

◯ Keeping the planets in orbit: Gravity

You learned about the force of gravity in Chapter 3. Most of the objects that we see are too small to create very large gravitational forces. Planets, however, are huge! They can create gravitational forces that hold objects close to the planet's surface – that's why we don't fall off the Earth! The Sun contains about 99% of all the matter in the Solar System. This huge mass creates a gravitational force that is enough to hold the planets in orbit. Each planet's orbit is a balance between the tendency of the planet to fly off into space and the pull on the planet due to the Sun's gravity.

> Planets orbit the Sun because of a balance between movement and the force of gravity.

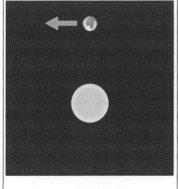

Without gravity a planet would speed off into space.

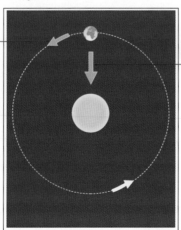

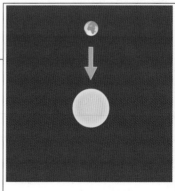

Without movement gravity would pull a planet into the Sun.

It's a bit like throwing a hammer!
There are some important points to note:

- The orbits are not quite circular. They are **elliptical**, with the Sun very close to the centre.
- The planets all travel around the Sun in the same direction.
- The dwarf planet Pluto has a very elliptical orbit and sometimes cuts inside the orbit of Neptune. This is one of the reasons why astronomers have doubts about whether Pluto is a true planet (but see pages 150–151).

The heavy ball tends to move away.

The wire acts like gravity and keeps the ball in orbit.

The planets' orbits are shown below:

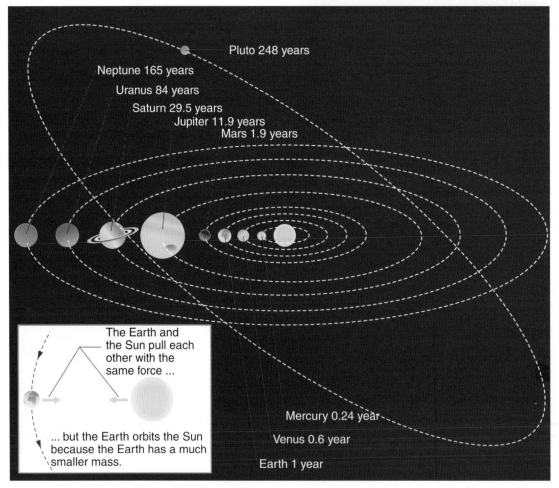

Pluto 248 years
Neptune 165 years
Uranus 84 years
Saturn 29.5 years
Jupiter 11.9 years
Mars 1.9 years

The Earth and the Sun pull each other with the same force ...

... but the Earth orbits the Sun because the Earth has a much smaller mass.

Mercury 0.24 year
Venus 0.6 year
Earth 1 year

The rules of gravity mean that:

- An inner planet will be pulled towards the Sun more strongly than an outer planet.
- A massive planet, such as Saturn, will be pulled towards the Sun more strongly than a small planet such as Neptune.

You can see that the time taken for a planet to orbit the Sun depends on its distance from the Sun. The bigger the orbit, the longer the planet takes to complete the orbit. One complete orbit by Neptune takes 165 Earth years!

Remember that gravity works both ways. The Earth attracts the Sun with exactly the same size of force as the Sun attracts the Earth. The Earth goes around the Sun (rather than the Sun around the Earth) because the Sun is so much more massive than the Earth.

Any object that completes an orbit around another one is called a **satellite**. For example, the Moon is a satellite of the Earth, and the Earth is a satellite of the Sun.

Go further

What is a comet?

Comets are bodies of rock and ice that move in orbit around the Sun. The orbits of comets are not all in the same plane, so the comets don't keep a fixed distance from the Earth. The famous Halley's Comet comes close to the Earth and Sun every 76 years. It speeds up when it approaches the Sun and slows down as it moves away again.

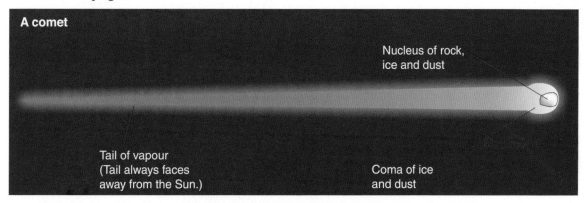

A comet

Nucleus of rock, ice and dust

Tail of vapour
(Tail always faces away from the Sun.)

Coma of ice and dust

1 Complete these sentences, using words from the list below:

    orbit   less   smaller   moving   larger   same   gravity

    Planets stay in orbit because they are _____ and because of the force of
    _____ . The force of gravity between two objects is exactly the _____ on both
    objects, but the _____ object orbits the _____ one. A satellite has _____ mass
    than a planet, so the satellite is in _____ around the planet.

2 Why is a Neptunian year much longer than a year on Earth?

Extension question

3 Halley's Comet was last seen in 1986. When will we be able to see it again?

4 (a) Use the table at the start of this chapter (features of the planets) to draw   **Working Scientifically**
        a graph of surface temperature against distance from the Sun.

    (b) What pattern does the graph show? Venus does not fit the general
        pattern. Try to find out why Venus is unusual in this way.

    (c) If the temperature of the Earth's surface were 40 °C higher, life could not
        survive. How far away from the Sun would the Earth have to be to have a
        temperature 40 °C higher than it is at present?

    (d) Imagine that another planet had been discovered, 2000 million kilometres
        from the Sun. What do you think its surface temperature would be?

◯ Artificial satellites help us to understand the Solar System

As you have learned, a satellite is an object that moves in an orbit around a larger body in the Solar System.

Movement in an orbit depends on a balance between the movement of the satellite and the gravity exerted by the larger body.

Some orbiting bodies are **natural satellites**, which means they have not been put in orbit by humans. The Earth is a natural satellite of the Sun, and the Moon is a natural satellite of the Earth. There are also hundreds of artificial satellites. These are objects made by humans that have been put into orbit by rockets or space shuttles.

Orbits for satellites

Satellites are held in orbit by the gravitational force of the Earth. The speed of the satellite depends on its height above the Earth. Satellites in low orbits travel faster than those in high orbits. These different orbits are described on the next page.

High elliptical orbits
- Move in and out as they orbit the Earth.
- Provide communications for people at the North Pole (signals from geostationary satellites over the equator do not reach the poles).

Polar orbits
- Study weather and help to predict storms.
- Provide navigation signals.
- Are not much use for communication as they go out of sight very quickly.

Low Earth orbits
- Have very short orbit times – 30 minutes or so.
- Used mainly for reconnaissance, they are close to the Earth's surface and so can provide very detailed photographs. They are widely used by the military to follow troop movements.

Geostationary orbit
- Move at a speed and height that makes them appear stationary above the Earth.
- Widely used in communications and for navigation and weather forecasting.

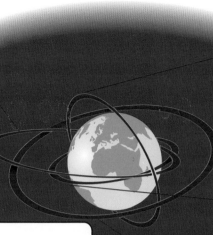

Artificial satellite

The body of the satellite contains measuring equipment.

Solar panels are used to provide energy. Fuel would be very heavy.

Geostationary satellites

A satellite that is 36 000 km above the Earth takes 24 hours to complete one orbit. This is precisely the same time that the Earth takes to turn once on its axis and, as a result, the satellite is always above the same place on the Earth's surface. This type of satellite – a geostationary satellite – behaves as though it is not moving, so it is very useful for sending information from one place to another. A **satellite dish** can be aimed at the satellite to receive signals and once it is correctly aimed, the dish never needs to be moved. See the diagram on the next page.

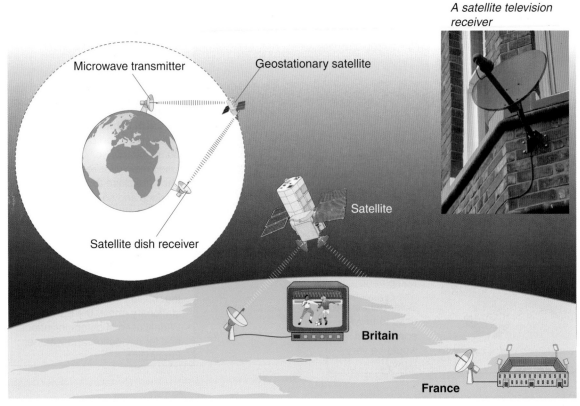

A satellite television receiver

Microwave transmitter

Geostationary satellite

Satellite

Satellite dish receiver

Britain

France

■ Communications are helped by geostationary satellites

Satellites and exploration of the Solar System

Satellites can help us to look at other planets. Telescopes placed on satellites can give a much clearer view of stars than can be obtained from telescopes on Earth because the images are not spoiled by dust and dirt in the Earth's atmosphere. The Hubble telescope is an example of this kind of instrument. The Hubble telescope can allow us to see seven times as far as we could from the Earth's surface.

■ Deployment of the Hubble space telescope from the space shuttle *Discovery* on 24 April 1990

Satellites and the global positioning system

The **global positioning system (GPS)** uses 24 satellites orbiting the Earth in six different orbits. A receiver on the ground can receive signals from at least four of the satellites at any one time. A small computer then allows the receiver to work out exactly where it is, to within 10 square metres. GPS is very valuable to the military, mountaineers, hill walkers and drivers. You will be familiar with the term 'satnav', which is short for satellite navigation. Drivers and walkers use these devices to tell them the best route to take, as well as where they are. Most modern smart phones have satellite navigation applications.

■ A satellite navigation system (satnav) in a car

Exercise 12.5: Satellites

1 Which type of satellite would be used by a satellite television network?
geostationary   low Earth orbit   high elliptical orbit   polar orbit

2 Give two uses for low Earth orbit satellites.

3 Why do you think that so many satellites are solar-powered?   ▌Working Scientifically

Extension question
4 Use the internet or textbooks to find out how satellites directly affect your life.

Exploration of space: A timeline

You will **not** need to remember the factual details about the exploration of space for your exam.

1966: The USA landed a robot spaceship, *Surveyor* 1, on the surface of the Moon. *Surveyor* 1 had sophisticated cameras on board, and was able to transmit detailed photographs of the Moon's surface back to Earth. The analysis of these photographs helped scientists to work out how humans could land safely on the Moon.

1961: Yuri Gagarin, a Russian cosmonaut, became the first human in space. Gagarin orbited the Earth once – it took almost two hours – in the spacecraft *Vostok* 1. Gagarin had to bail out of *Vostok* 1 using a parachute, as the spacecraft could not be designed to land softly!

The first woman in space was also Russian – Valentina Tereshkova. She orbited the Earth 48 times on board *Vostok* 6.

1959: Russia landed a space probe (*Luna* 2) on the Moon, although the landing impact was so great any human on board would have been killed!

1957: The real start of the Space Age – Russia launched the first satellite into space. *Sputnik* (which means 'satellite' in Russian) weighed about 83 kg and is believed to have orbited Earth at an altitude of about 250 km. It had two radio transmitters that emitted 'beeps' that could be heard by radios around the globe. *Sputnik* burned up upon re-entry on 3 January 1958. Also in 1957, the Russians launched a satellite carrying Laika, a dog (Laika means 'barker' in Russian), which therefore became the first living organism to orbit the Earth.

1950: The USA first launched a two-part rocket. The *Bumper* rocket could reach then-record altitudes of almost 400 km. This *Bumper* was used primarily for testing rocket systems and for research on the upper atmosphere: it carried instruments that allowed it to measure factors including air temperature and cosmic ray impacts.

1949: Albert II, a rhesus monkey, became the first monkey in space. He was launched on a modified V-2 rocket, and reached a height about 140 km above the Earth. Albert II did not complete an orbit of the Earth, so the information collected about the possibilities of animals surviving in space was quite limited.

1942: The German V-2 was the first rocket to reach the boundary of space (100 km above the Earth's surface). The rocket was designed by Wernher von Braun with the intention of sending explosive warheads to the UK: von Braun later worked with NASA as a co-designer of the rocket systems used to launch animals into space and to send robots to the Moon.

1969: Neil Armstrong and Buzz Aldrin, two American astronauts, became the first men on the Moon (or, indeed, on any other celestial body). The spaceship that carried them to the Moon, *Apollo* 11, travelled 250 000 miles to the Moon and back. As part of the Apollo series of Moon explorations, a total of 6 missions landed there with 12 astronauts walking (and, on the fourth, fifth and sixth missions, driving the Lunar Rover) on the Moon's surface.

1973: The Russian space probe *Mars* 2 explored Mars. The probe had two parts: one stayed in orbit for a year and the other attempted to land on the surface of the planet. The landing attempt was not a success, and the lander was destroyed when its parachute failed.

1981: The space shuttle was launched for the first time. This 'space vehicle' was designed to be reused, in an attempt to reduce the enormous costs of space exploration. At launch, the space shuttle consisted of the shuttle stack, which includes a dark orange-coloured external fuel tank, two white, slender solid rocket boosters and the orbiter vehicle, which contained the crew and payload. In 1986, the space shuttle *Challenger* exploded shortly after launch, following a fuel leak. All seven astronauts on board were killed – a reminder of the dangers of space travel. In 2003, space shuttle *Columbia* burned up on re-entry to the Earth's atmosphere. The final space shuttle mission ended on 21 July 2011.

1994/1995: The longest single human spaceflight is that of Valeriy Polyakov, who left Earth on 8 January **1994**, and didn't return until 22 March **1995** (a total of 437 days 17 hours 58 minutes 16 seconds aboard MIR).

1986: Construction of the MIR space station began. MIR was built up in sections, carried into space, and then bolted together – construction was completed in 1996, and MIR continued to be inhabited until 2001. In 1991 Helen Sharman became the first British astronaut in space when she spent eight days on MIR.

2000: The first permanent crew moved into the ISS (International Space Station). This is so large that it can be seen from the Earth with the unaided eye! It contains several advanced laboratories, working, for example, on the effects of reduced gravity on animals and plants. The ISS has been built and is maintained by space agencies from the USA, Russia, Europe and Japan.

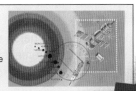

2001: The American millionaire Dennis Tito became the first space tourist when he paid for a visit to the ISS. He spent a week in orbit, and the trip cost him $20 million

2003: After four unmanned tests, *Shenzhou* 5 launched, carrying Chinese astronaut Yang Liwei and making the People's Republic of China the third country to put a human being into space through its own endeavours. In 2008, China successfully completed the *Shenzhou* 7 mission, making it the third country to have the capability to conduct a spacewalk.

2011: NASA launched its Mars Science Laboratory (MSL) mission to Mars. This mission successfully landed *Curiosity*, a Mars rover, in Gale Crater in August 2012. Objectives of the mission include investigating Mars' climate and geology to assess its habitability and collecting data for a later manned mission.

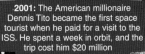

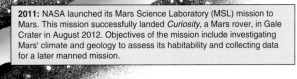

◯ Exploration of space

During the past three or four centuries human scientists have investigated many of the problems that affect life on the planet Earth – in the last 60 years, however, scientists have extended their investigations to include the space beyond planet Earth.

These are some of the methods that astronomers have used:

- Observations made by telescopes from Earth's surface.
- A variety of space missions have sent satellites carrying instruments capable of making measurements in space and sending this information back to powerful computers on Earth.
- The design of robots and space vehicles, and rockets to carry them, allowing exploration of the surface of other planets.
- The construction of rockets and life-support systems that have allowed people to visit and explore other parts of the Solar System.

> A brief timeline of some of these investigations and discoveries is shown on the previous pages.

Since the successful 1957 launch of *Sputnik*, the first artificial satellite, into orbit around Earth, more and more countries have joined the space age. Currently, scientists believe that the USA, Russia, China, India (and even the Isle of Man!) might have the capability to send humans into space. What began as a 'space race' – in which the United States and the then Soviet Union raced each other to demonstrate superiority in space technology (possibly with military reasons) – has developed into a co-operative effort to find answers in space.

Because of the challenge and expense of space travel for humans, robotic exploration of space is much more practical. Robots are ideal for space research because they can be designed and built with one particular mission in mind. They are able to withstand the harsh conditions of space (no oxygen, for example) and to survive the extremely long missions.

There are different types of different specialised robotic missions:

- A flyby collects information as the spacecraft travels past the target object, possibly on a longer mission. For example, the Cassini-Huygens mission did a flyby of Venus and Jupiter while on its way to visit Saturn and its moons.
- An **orbiter** allows a longer period of study as the spacecraft travels in repeated orbit around the object under study.
- A **probe** passes down through a planet's atmosphere to study what it is made of. For example, the Huygens probe of the Cassini-Huygens mission studied the atmosphere of Saturn's moon Titan.
- **Landers** gather data about the surfaces of the celestial objects on which they land. **Rovers** also study the surfaces of objects, but they are mobile and thus can examine a greater area.

Each of these missions involves the efforts of many different scientists and engineers, often communicating with one another from different countries.

Glossary

Acceleration   how fast the speed of something is changing.

Air resistance   friction between the air and a moving object (sometimes called drag).

Ammeter   an instrument for measuring electrical current.

Ampere (A)   the unit of electrical current (often shortened to amps).

Amplitude   the size of a vibration, determines how loud or soft a sound will be.

AND circuit   a circuit that requires two switches in series to be closed for current to flow.

Angle of incidence   the angle between the normal and the incident ray.

Angle of reflection   the angle between the normal and the reflected ray.

Appliance   a device that can change electrical energy into a form of energy that is useful to us.

Artificial satellites   objects made by humans that have been put into orbit.

Asteroid   a large lump of rock out in the solar system.

Axis   an imaginary line between the North and South Poles of the Earth.

Battery   a mobile source of electrical energy, made up of one or more cells.

Cell   a chemical source of electrical energy. Cells may be connected in series to make up a battery.

Centre of gravity   the point that the weight of an object seems to pass through.

Circuit   the complete route from the positive terminal to the negative terminal of a power source.

Circuit symbols   symbols representing different components in a circuit diagram.

Comet   bodies of rock and ice in orbit around the Sun.

Compass   an instrument that can measure the direction of the Earth's magnetic field.

Component   one part of an electrical circuit.

Conductor   a material that allows electrical energy to pass through it.

Core   an iron bar that may be placed inside a solenoid to form a powerful electromagnet.

Current   a flow of electrons/charge.

Diffuse scattering   the scattering of light rays passing through a translucent material.

Dissipated   spread out from the place of production.

Eclipse   when either the Moon or the Sun is hidden from viewers on the Earth.

Efficiency   a way of comparing the energy given out by a device with the energy it uses high efficiency means very little energy is wasted.

Electromagnet   a magnet formed when electric current passes through a wire.

Electromagnetic spectrum   the complete range of electromagnetic waves.

Electron   a tiny particle that has a negative charge. Electrons can flow through conductors.

Elliptical   shaped like an oval.

Energy   the capacity for doing work (a measure of work done or able to be done).

Force   a push or a pull   it has both size and direction.

Force meter (newton meter)   an instrument used to measure the size of a force.

Fossil fuel   remains of long-dead animals and plants.

Frequency   the number of vibrations in a certain time determines the pitch of a sound.

Friction   a force that tries to stop two things sliding over one another.

Fuel   a store of energy that can go through a reaction to release the energy.

Fuse   a component that breaks a circuit if the current in a wire becomes too great.

Galaxy   a collection of millions of stars.

Generator   a device that changes kinetic energy into electrical energy.

Geostationary   an orbit that keeps a satellite in a fixed position above the Earth.

Geothermal   thermal energy from the ground.

Gravity   a force of attraction between any two masses.

Hertz (Hz)   the unit of frequency – number of cycles per second.

Hydraulic pressure   pressure transmitted through a liquid.

Insulator   a material that prevents the flow of electrical energy.

Joule (J)   a unit of energy (energy exerted when a force of one newton is applied over a displacement of one metre).

Kinetic energy   energy possessed by moving particles.

Law of Conservation of Energy   energy cannot be created or destroyed (although it can be changed from one form into another).

Law of Moments   a situation where moments are balanced.

Lead   a wire that can connect different components in a circuit.

Lever   any rigid body that is able to turn about a pivot.

Light year   a unit of distance in the Universe – the distance travelled by light in one year.

Lubricant   a substance that reduces friction between two objects.

Luminous   a light source that produces and gives off its own light.

Lunar month   the time taken for the Moon to complete one orbit of the Earth.

Machine   a device that can use energy to carry out work.

Magnet   a material that can put a pulling force on any object that contains iron.

Magnetic   attracted by a magnet.

Magnetic field   a region where there is a magnetic force.

Magnetism   the pulling force between a magnet and a magnetic object.

Mains   a source of electrical energy that is delivered to a house or factory from power lines.

Mass   how much matter an object contains.

Medium   the material that a sound wave travels through.

Milky Way   the galaxy that includes our Solar System.

Moment   the strength of a turning effect of a force – it equals the force × the distance to the pivot.

Moon   a large body orbiting a planet.

Non-renewable resource   an energy source that is in finite supply, so will run out.

Nuclear power   energy released from the nucleus of an atom.

OR circuit   a circuit that allows current to flow if either of two switches in series is on.

Orbit   the path followed by one object as it travels around another one in space. The word can also be used as a verb i.e. *to* orbit means to travel around an object in space.

Parallel circuit   a circuit that contains junctions where the electrical pathway divides or branches.

Pitch   how high or low a sound is – affected by the frequency of the sound.

Pivot   the point around which something turns.

Plane mirror   a reflecting surface that is flat.

Planet   a celestial body moving in orbit around a star.

Poles   the different ends of an electrical component – one will be positive and the other will be negative; or the ends of a magnet – north-seeking and south-seeking.

Pressure   force divided by the area that the force is acting on.

Prism   a glass triangle that can split white light into its seven different colours.

Reaction force   an upward force that supports a body.

Reflection   the bouncing of light or sound waves from a surface.

Reflector   an object that is bright because light from another source can bounce off it.

Refraction   the bending of light or sound waves when it moves from one medium to another of different density.

Relative motion   the calculation of the speed of movement of an object with regard to some other moving object.

Renewable energy resource   an energy source that can be replaced naturally, and so will not run out. (Not the same as reusable!)

Resistance   a measure of how difficult it is for electrical current to flow through a component.

Resistor   a component with a known resistance.

Sankey diagram   a picture that shows what happens to the energy input to a machine.

Satellite   an object that moves around a larger mass in the Solar System.

Seasons   the four divisions of the year (spring, summer, autumn and winter) resulting from the tilting of the Earth's in relation to the Sun.

Series circuit   an electrical circuit with all of the components joined in a single loop.

Shadow   an area formed when an object gets in the way of rays of light.

Short circuit   the easiest route in an electrical circuit.

Solar System   the eight planets, including Earth, their moons, dwarf planets and other smaller bodies in orbit around the Sun.

Solenoid   a coil of wire that forms part of an electromagnet.

Sound wave   a pattern of vibrations carrying sound energy through the air.

Spectrum (plural: spectra)   a range of colours of light.

Speed   how fast an object is moving – distance travelled divided by time taken.

Star   a large, hot ball of glowing gas.

Switch   a device that controls the flow of current in a circuit.

Temperature   a measure of how concentrated an object's thermal (internal) energy is.

Terminals   the positive and negative ends of a power source.

Thermal conduction   movement of thermal energy through a medium.

Thermal energy   giving an object more of this makes it hotter.

Thermal insulation   prevention of the movement of thermal energy.

Thermocouple   two wires twisted together that can be used as a very sensitive thermometer.

Thermometer   an instrument for measuring temperature.

Transform   the change of energy from one form to another, e.g. electrical energy into thermal energy.

Truth table   used to show the action of switches in AND and OR circuits.

Turbine   a rotary engine in which kinetic energy is converted into mechanical energy by causing a blade to rotate.

Universe   all of space containing everything that exists.

Upthrust   a push of water against an object floating in it.

Vacuum   a space containing no air particles.

Vibration   a pattern of movement, up-and-down or side-to-side.

Virtual image   an image that appears to be behind a mirror.

Visible spectrum   the part of the electromagnetic spectrum that we can see.

Volt (V)   the unit of electrical 'push'.

Wave   the pattern of energy movement from one place to another.

Wavelength   the distance between two successive peaks of a wave.

Weight   the force of gravity that pulls an object towards another object (usually towards the Earth).

Work   any process that uses up energy.

Year   the time taken for the Earth to complete one orbit of the Sun.

Index